FINANCE

BUSINESS MANAGEMENT ENGLISH SERIES

Comfort, J. and N. Brieger
Marketing

Brieger, N. and J. Comfort
Production and Operations

Brieger, N. and J. Comfort
Personnel

Brieger, N. and J. Comfort
Language Reference for Business English

Other ESP titles of interest include:

Brieger, N. and J. Comfort
*Business Contacts**

Brieger, N. and A. Cornish
*Secretarial Contacts**

Brieger, N. and J. Comfort
*Technical Contacts**

Brieger, N. and J. Comfort
*Social Contacts**

Brieger, N. and J. Comfort
Business Issues

Davies, S. *et al.*
*Bilingual Handbooks of Business
Correspondence and Communication*

McGovern, J. and J. McGovern
*Bank On Your English**

McKellen, J. and M. Spooner
*New Business Matters**

Palstra, R.
*Telephone English**

Palstra, R.
Telex English

Pote, M. *et al.*
*A Case for Business English**

* Includes audio cassette(s)

bme *BUSINESS MANAGEMENT ENGLISH*

FINANCE

Jeremy Comfort
and
Nick Brieger

Longman

Pearson Education Limited
Edinburgh Gate
Harlow
Essex
CM20 2JE
England
and Associated Companies throughout the World

www.longman-elt.com

First published by Prentice Hall Ltd 1992
This edition published by Pearson Education Limited 1999
Fourth impression 2000

Typeset by Keyboard Services, Luton
Printed in Malaysia GPS

Library of Congress Cataloging-in-Publication Data

Comfort, Jeremy.
    Finance / Jeremy Comfort and Nick Brieger
        p.   cm. – (Business management English series) (English
    language teaching)
    ISBN 0–13–093444–5
    1. Finance – Study and teaching.   2. English language – Business
English.   3. English language – Study and teaching – Foreign speakers.
    4. Finance – Terminology.   I. Title.   II. Series.   III. Series:
English language teaching.
    HG152.C66   1991
    658.15'014 – dc20   91–19206
                                                                      CIP

British Library Cataloguing in Publication Data

Comfort, Jeremy
    Finance. – (Business management English series)
    I. Title   II. Brieger, Nick   III. Series
    658.15

    ISBN 0–13–093444–5

Contents

Introduction

The Business Management English (BME) series comprises four professional content books:

Marketing
Finance
Production and Operations
Personnel

and also *Language Reference for Business English*, which acts as a language and communication reference for the other four titles.

Rationale

The rationale behind the BME series is to bring together training material in:

- key management disciplines.
- language knowledge, and
- communication skills

The material is thus designed for:

- specialists who need to develop language and communication skills within their professional areas, and
- non-specialists who wish to extend their knowledge of management areas and develop their language and communication skills.

Finance

Targets and objectives

This book is aimed at practitioners and students of financial management: people who need to communicate in English within the increasingly international world of business management. More specifically the material is targeted at non-native speakers of English, with at least an intermediate level in the language, who need to:

- increase their effectiveness in reading and listening in this subject area,
- develop speaking and writing skills around this subject area,
- extend their active vocabulary of both specific financial terms and more general business English, and
- transfer this knowledge of the language to their own work or study situation.

Organisation of materials

The book and its accompanying cassette are divided into three: Study Material, Key and Glossary.

STUDY MATERIAL

The Study Material comprises seven units, each of which is divided into two sections (A and B). Each section (A and B) is divided into two parts.

Part 1 is based on a reading task; Part 2 on a listening task. Each part contains the following activities:

1. *Warm-up*
   Questions designed as orientation for the following reading/listening task.

2. *Reading/Listening*
   An input text, together with a task.

3. *Comprehension/interpretation*
   Detailed questions about the input text.

4. *Language focus*
   Language practice exercises – a background explanation is given in *Language Reference for Business English*.

5. *Word study*
   Language exercises to develop professional, business and idiomatic vocabulary.

6. *Transfer*
   A speaking or writing communication task which encourages the user to transfer the information presented into his/her own field.

KEY

This comprises:

- Tapescripts of the listening extracts.
- Answers to the following activities from the Study Material:
  2. *Reading/Listening* task.
  3. *Comprehension/interpretation* questions.
  4. *Language focus* exercises.
  5. *Word study* exercises.
- Information for the communication activities, where needed.

GLOSSARY
A five hundred word dictionary of financial management. The words have been selected on the basis of frequent usage in this subject area. They are not confined to words used in the book. Simple definitions are followed by an example of usage, where appropriate.

Using a unit – activities in each part

1. Warm-up
The questions here will help you to orientate yourself toward the tasks which follow. They encourage you to think about and discuss the subject area.

2. Reading/Listening

(i) *Reading*
Each text has been selected to focus on a key area of professional interest. There is always a task to perform either as you read or just after. This makes the process active. In order to develop your reading skills, you should:

- skim through the text to identify major themes and
- scan through the relevant paragraphs to complete the task.

Then check your answers with the Key. If they are wrong, read the appropriate section again. The reading task is best done for homework/individual study; the answers can then be discussed in class.

(ii) *Listening*
Each text has been developed to focus on a key area of professional interest. Again there is always a task to perform as you listen to the cassette. In order to develop your listening skills, you should:

- listen all the way through first time, then
- listen again, stopping the cassette to write your answers.

Finally, check your answers with the Key.

3. Comprehension/interpretation
The questions have been developed to:

- check your detailed understanding, and
- encourage you to think more deeply about the subject.

You may need to read/listen again to answer the questions. If you are working in a class, discuss your answers. Finally, check the Key. As you will see, sometimes there is no 'correct' answer.

4. Language focus

This activity focuses on developing your language knowledge. You can do these exercises in class or on a self-study basis. Refer to *Language Reference for Business English* if you need further information. When you have completed an exercise, check the answers in the Key.

5. Word study

This activity concentrates on developing your word power. You can do this activity in class or on a self-study basis. The answers are in the Key. You may wish to check the Reading or Listening passage to see how the words are used.

6. Transfer

This activity develops your language and communication skills. It is best done in pairs or small groups. You will sometimes find additional information in the Key.

Acknowledgements

The authors would like to acknowledge the advice and support of Martin Robinson (Leeds Business School), who gave invaluable assistance on the financial content of the book, and their colleagues at York Associates, who gave them the time and space to complete and trial this book.

The publishers and authors would like to acknowledge with thanks the following copyright permissions:

Unit 5
'Flying in the face of accounting convention', Richard Waters, *Financial Times*.
'Auditors may assume role of whistle blower', David Waller, *Financial Times*.

Unit 6
Corporation Tax: Principles of Financial Management, Levy and Sarnat (1988), Prentice Hall.
'Chaos more likely than harmony', Richard Waters, *Financial Times*.

Unit 7
'Wrong figures lead to wrong decisions', David Waller, *Financial Times*.

STUDY MATERIAL

UNIT 1
The financial climate

Part 1: World economic climate

1 *Warm-up*

1.1   How important is the state of the world economy for the financial state of an
      international business?
1.2   Do financial managers need to interpret trends in the world economy?

2 *Reading*

Read the following article 'World economic pointers are discouraging' (June 1990).
As you read it, indicate economic trends in Chart 1.1.

The world economy appears to have taken a turn for the worse this year.

Last year's surprisingly strong growth in the developed world and the newly
industrialising countries of Asia has given way to fears that the current seven year
recovery from the recession of the early '80s may be about to end in the familiar cycle
of stop–go.

Inflation has returned to haunt the major industrial economies, forcing interest
rates higher from the lows set after the global stock market crash of 1987.

The international debt crisis has flared up again reminding us that Latin America
and other parts of the developing world have largely missed out on the growing
prosperity of the 1980s.

Serious doubts have resurfaced about the viability of the economic policies
pursued by the US. The International Monetary Fund (IMF) warned recently that
continuing strong domestic demand could trigger a new jump in the US current

account balance of payments deficit, with the attendant risk of a sudden drop in the dollar's value and a further twist to the international interest-rate spiral.

The state of international trade remains a worry. The discontent in the US about the imbalance of trade with Japan could lead to a return to protectionist measures.

This uncertain view of the world was reflected in the IMF's latest World Economic Outlook report, at the beginning of April. On first reading it appeared to offer some hope that the industrial world can achieve a soft landing from its present overheated state.

The IMF projected a slight decline in the rate of output growth in the industrial countries, to 2.9% next year from 3.3% this year. Consumer-price inflation was projected to fall next year to an average of 3.5%, after rising to 3.8% this year.

But the IMF projections also foresaw a marked deterioration of the global current account imbalance. They said that the US current account deficit could jump to $156bn next year from $139bn this year. It projected a rise in Japan's current account surplus increasing to $93bn from $84bn this year. Similarly, West Germany's surplus was forecast to increase from $49bn to $51bn.

Such developments could cause international investors to scale down their demand for US dollar assets. That, in the IMF's view, 'would involve a significant risk of instability in financial markets, accompanied by high inflation and a slowdown in growth'.

Chart 1.1 World economic trends
   (↗ upwards trend, ↘ downwards trend)

Interest rates	
Output	
Inflation	
US c/a deficit	
Japan c/a surplus	
West Germany c/a surplus	

3 Comprehension/interpretation

3.1   What is meant by a stop–go cycle?

3.2   What is the international debt crisis?

3.3   Why should strong domestic demand lead to a further increase in US c/a deficit?

3.4   What sort of protectionist measures could be imposed on Japan?

3.5   What is meant by a 'soft landing'?

4 Language focus

4.1 Tense review (see Unit 11 in *Language Reference for Business English*)

Look at the following sentences taken from the Reading passage:

'The world economy *appears to have taken* a turn for the worse this year.'
'Inflation *has returned* to haunt the major industrial economies . . .'

Now complete the following sentences by putting the bracketed verb into the right tense:

1. Inflation _____ (increase) steadily this year.
2. Unemployment _____ (peak) last year and since then *has gone* (go down).
3. As the international debt crisis *grows* (grow), the world economy *becomes* (become) more unstable.
4. The IMF *carried* (carry out) a study last year. In this study they *projected* (project) a decline in GNP in most countries.
5. The world economy *seems* (seem) to *be going* (go) into a decline.
6. If Japan's current account surplus _____ (increase) further it will cause even more instability in the world economy.
7. The state of international trade _____ (remain) a worry. Projections for the rest of the nineties _____ (bring) very little hope.
8. We *are* (study) the effect of the fall in the dollar's value at the moment.
9. We would have preferred more stability if that *had* (be) possible.
10. For more than ten years the value of the US dollar *has* (fall). Before that, it *was* (be) one of the stronger currencies.

5 Word study

5.1 Group the following words/expressions as either upward trend (U) or downward trend (D).

growth рост   decline снижение
подъём recovery   fall падение
рост скачок jump   rise повышаться
провал drop   increase увеличивать.

5.2 Use the information contained in Chart 1.2 to complete the sentences below.

Chart 1.2 Growth rates

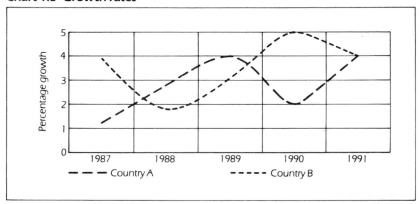

1. During the period 1987–89, country A's economy _grew_ steadily. *постоянно*
2. In 1990, it _dropped_ from 4 per cent to 2 per cent but then _increased_ the following year when it _rose_ back to 4 per cent.
3. Country B's economy _declined_ from 1987 to 1988, then output started to _increase_.
4. It reached 5 per cent in 1990 and since then it has _fallen_ slightly to 4 per cent. *достигло*

6 *Transfer*

Use the information in the article and the language above to present a summary of the world economic climate.

Part 2: Key indicators *ключевой показатели*

1 *Warm-up*

Which key economic indicators need to be most carefully monitored?

2 *Listening*

Listen to the sales manager giving a presentation about domestic and export sales. As you listen, complete the graphs shown in Charts 1.3 and 1.4.

Chart 1.3 Domestic and export sales

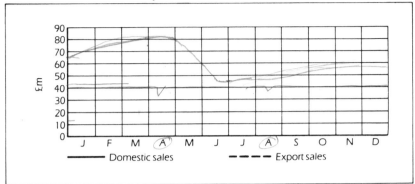

Chart 1.4 Currency rates and inflation

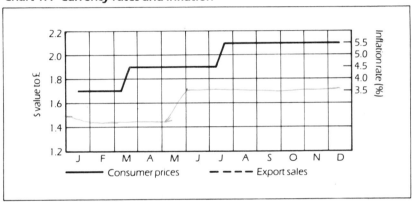

3 Comprehension/interpretation

3.1   Why should a British company invoice its export goods in US dollars?
3.2   What reasons could explain the changes in the value of the dollar?
3.3   Why is there a delay factor as far as the customers are concerned?
3.4   Why should a rise in interest rates affect domestic sales?

4 Language focus

4.1 Present perfect and past simple (see Units 3 and 5 in *Language Reference for Business English*)

Look at the following sentences taken from the Listening passage:

> 'Domestic sales . . . *have remained* pretty constant for most of the year . . .'
> 'They . . . *rose* in the first quarter to a new record of £82 million.'

Now complete the following sentences by putting the verb in brackets into either the present perfect or past simple:

1. At the end of last year the dollar *stood* (stand) at 1.5.
2. Last January the dollar *fell* (fall) to a new low of 1.45.
3. Since then it *'s been* (be) pretty stable.
4. As you can see on this graph, I *'ve plotted* (plot) domestic and export sales.
5. Export sales *fluctuated* (fluctuate) pretty wildly.
6. We *haven't seen* yet (not see) the full effect of the declining dollar.
7. Last quarter we *saw* (see) one of the best results.
8. We *'ve noticed* already (notice) a slight drop in orders.
9. The low profit margins *were* (reflect) in last year's figures.
10. We *received* (receive) two big orders so far this quarter.

4.2 Past reference (see Unit 63 in *Language Reference for Business English*)

Look at the following sentences taken from the Listening passage:

> 'They recovered a bit *over the next few months* . . .'
> 'Now, *at the end of last year*, the dollar stood at around 1.5.'

Now complete the following sentences with one of the following time 'prepositions':

over   **at**   **during**   **since**   **for**   **in**   **ago**

1. *For* the last few months, sales have been disappointing.
2. We have been expecting an upturn *since* the beginning of the year.
3. *At* the end of last year, there was a sudden downturn.
4. He was appointed finance director two years *ago* and *since* then he has reduced the staff by 200.
5. We went through a difficult period *over* the middle of April.
6. The computer system crashed *during* the holidays.
7. We have raised prices in line with inflation *for* three years.
8. The dips in the price index happened *in* April and July.

5 Word study

Match the terms below to the reference points marked on Chart 1.5.

1. solid line *сплошную линию*
2. broken line *прерыв линию*
3. dotted line *пунктирн. линию*
4. to rise steadily *↑ постоянно*
5. to level off *выровнять*

6. to remain constant *оставаться постоя…*
7. to reach a plateau *достигнуть*
8. to fluctuate wildly *менаться дико*
9. to dip slightly *↓ медленно*
10. to fall dramatically *↓ резко*

Chart 1.5

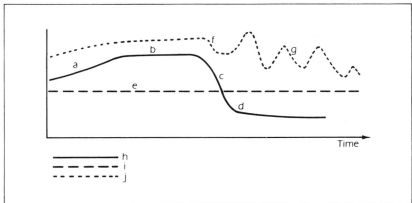

6 Transfer

PAIR WORK (Partner B turn to the Key)

A: (i) Describe the following graph (Chart 1.6a) to your partner so that s/he can plot it accurately.

   (ii) Listen to your partner's presentation and plot the information on the blank graph (Chart 1.6b).

Chart 1.6a Inflation rate

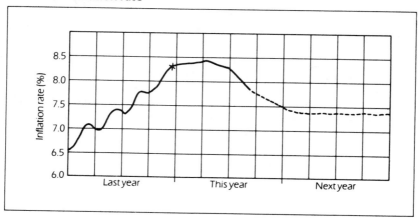

Chart 1.6b

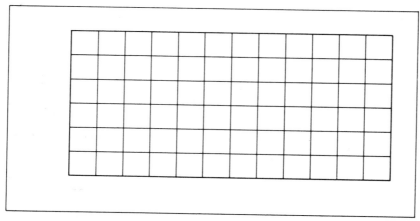

UNIT 2
Funding the business

Section A: Sources of funds

Part 1: Gearing

1 Warm-up

1.1 What sources can an entrepreneur go to in order to start up a new business?

1.2 What are the advantages for an entrepreneur to finance his/her new business from his/her own personal funds?

2 Reading

Read the passage below about gearing. As you read it, complete Chart 2.1.

To ensure a company's long-term survival and prosperity, finance managers need to make decisions about the *gearing* of the company. Gearing is the relationship between equity capital invested in the business and long-term debt. The higher the gearing (in other words, the greater the proportion of long-term debt), the more exposed the company is in times of economic difficulty.

The first form of equity is owner's capital. This is the most exposed form of capital since a return is received only after all other calls on a company's profits have been satisfied. In an extreme case – bankruptcy – the owner's equity will be repaid only after everyone else, including employees, creditors, banks etc., has received what they are owed. On the other hand, in successful times, the owners have a claim on all the net profit of the company.

An owner does not need to rely on his or her own funds. S/he can go to other sources of equity finance. There are three main sources: firstly *venture capital:* this is usually provided by venture firms interested in financing high-growth companies. However, the provider usually demands a much faster and higher rate of return than an owner would expect from his/her own capital. On the other hand, the venture capital company does not usually interfere in the running of the company.

Another source of equity finance is the *unlisted securities market* – sometimes called the second or third market. This has the advantage of allowing a company to raise money from outside investors without losing much control of the company.

The last source is available only to large companies – the *Stock Exchange.* If a company gains a listing on the Stock Exchange, this will provide the long-term opportunity of raising capital by issuing fresh shares. However, at least 25 per cent of the equity must be in public hands – thereby reducing the control of the original owners.

Companies prepared to increase their gearing can raise capital through long-term loans. They can go to sources such as the clearing banks, merchant banks and even pension funds. However, in all three cases they will usually secure their debt over the fixed assets of the business and, of course, interest must be paid, usually linked to bank base rate.

In times of prosperity, a high gearing will give the owners a much better return as net profits will be a much higher percentage of equity even after interest payments on the long-term debt. However, in harder times, the owner's earnings will drop dramatically as interest payments soak up most of the company's profits.

Chart 2.1

	Sources of funds	Advantages/disadvantages
Low gearing	(i) Owner's capital	
	(ii)	
	(iii)	
	(iv)	
High gearing	Long-term loans	

3 Comprehension/interpretation

Analyse the gearing of these two companies and comment on the dangers.

	Company A	Company B
Equity	$100,000	$250,000
Long-term debt	300,000	150,000
Profits	50,000	30,000
Interest paid (10%)	30,000	15,000
Earnings	20,000	15,000

4 Language focus

4.1 Comparison of adjectives (see Unit 50 in *Language Reference for Business English*)

Look at the following sentences taken from the Reading passage:

'This is the *most exposed* form of capital . . .'
'The provider usually demands a *much faster* and *higher* rate of return *than* an owner . . .'

Now complete the sentences with the correct comparative or superlative form of the adjective in brackets.

1. It's much _____ (hard) to raise money on the Stock Exchange.
2. Increasing owner's capital is the _____ (risky) way of raising money for investment.
3. The banks will be _____ (cautious) than the securities markets.
4. Interest rates are much _____ (high) this year than last.
5. The _____ (safe) method of increasing working capital is to plough back profits.
6. A fixed-term loan is _____ (flexible) than a fluctuating overdraft.
7. On the other hand, a medium-term loan is _____ (easy) to control than a fluctuating overdraft.
8. Venture capital is much _____ (difficult) to raise than we are led to believe.
9. The Stock Exchange rules are much _____ (formal) than the USM.
10. Expansion is _____ (attractive) in times of low interest rates.

4.2 Contrast (see Unit 72 in *Language Reference for Business English*)

Look at the following sentences taken from the Reading passage.

'*On the other hand*, in successful times, the owners have a claim on all the profit of the company.'
'*However*, at least 25% of the equity must be in public hands . . .'

Now weigh advantages against disadvantages using the following prompts:

Subject	Advantage	Disadvantage
Sutton Savings Bank	Small and friendly	No solid experience
First National Bank	Solid, good track record	Very impersonal
Trust Financial Services	Attractive venture capital scheme	High interest rates
Welcome Investments Ltd	Low interest rates	Low maximum capital sums

1. Sutton Savings Bank *offers a small and friendly service. On the other hand,*
    _____
2. First National Bank _____
3. Trust Financial Services _____
4. Welcome Investments Ltd _____

5 *Word study*

One way to extend your active vocabulary is to generate other forms of a base word (usually the verb). For example:

> verb: **to compete**   noun: **competition**   noun (agent): **competitor**

NOTE: Not all verbs have a noun agent form.

Generate other forms from these verbs:

Verbs	Nouns (concept)	Nouns (agent)
to survive	_____	a _____
to prosper	_____	
to bankrupt (to go bankrupt)	_____	
to provide	_____	a _____
to interfere	_____	
to invest	_____	an _____
to secure	_____	
to earn	_____	
to own	_____	an _____

6 *Transfer*

Use Chart 2.1 and the language above to present the financing options open to an entrepreneur wanting to start up his/her own business.

Part 2: Negotiating a loan

1 Warm-up

What aspects of a company's business will a lender be interested in? How will he decide whether to lend money or not?

2 Listening

Listen to the meeting between a bank manager and one of her customers. As you listen, complete the information below:

Reason for loan: _____
Amount of loan: _____
Term of loan: _____
Interest rate: _____
Current instalment: _____
Security: type: _____
        market value: _____
Turnover: _____
Profits: _____
Assets: _____
Liabilities: _____

3 Comprehension/interpretation

3.1 How could the firm raise £50,000 towards the cost of the property?
3.2 What are the firm's projections for turnover and profits?
3.3 What is its current overdraft?
3.4 Who does it owe money to?

4 Language focus

4.1 Asking questions – direct forms (see Unit 38 in *Language Reference for Business English*)

Look at the following questions taken from the Listening passage:

    'How much are they asking for it?'
    'Are you looking for a loan to cover the total price?'

Now ask questions for the following answers:

1. A: We'd like to borrow £20,000.
2. A: It's for a new computer system.
3. A: Yes, we've had three quotations. This is the best.
4. A: No, it's not the full amount. It's actually costing £25,000.
5. A: We'd like to repay it over five years.

6. A: Yes, I realise the total interest payment will be high.
7. A: Well, we thought our existing security arrangements would cover it.
8. A: Well, you have second mortgages on two partners' houses.
9. A: At present values, I'd say £200,000 – £100,000 for each.
10. A: No, that's all. We'd be grateful if the paperwork could go through as soon as possible.

4.2   Questions – statement type (see Unit 38 in *Language Reference for Business English*)

Look at the following questions taken from the Listening passage:

> '*But ideally you'd like to borrow the full £300,000 (wouldn't you)?*'
> '*Perhaps you can leave the figures with me?*'

Now change the following direct questions into leading (statement) questions. Question tags are optional.

1. Would you like to extend the repayment period?
2. Have you got any financial problems at the moment?
3. Do you see any improvement in your cash flow?
4. Can you offer any form of collateral?
5. Could you tell me if your current liabilities are higher than usual?
6. Would you mind telling me whether you intend to reduce the payment periods?

5 Word study

Match the words/expressions on the left with an appropriate combination on the right, to make an idiomatic phrase:

1. short of	a. figures
2. a major drain	b. the wrong side
3. close to	c. investment
4. our line of	d. space
5. to come down	e. business
6. a firm of	f. calculation
7. to stray	g. on cash
8. up-to-date	h. in favour of
9. rough	i. the limit
10. sound	j. your size

6 Transfer

DISCUSSION

Use the information and the language above to discuss the loan. Would you lend the money? If so, why? If not, why not?

Section B: Management of working capital

Part 1: Types and uses of working capital

1 Warm-up

1.1 What is the difference between equity capital and working capital?

1.2 How can a company calculate its needs for working capital?

2 Reading

Read the following extract which describes the types and uses of working capital. As you read it, complete the classification shown in Chart 2.2.

Profitability is determined in part by the way in which a company manages its working capital. Basically there will be a drop in profits if working capital is raised without a corresponding rise in production or margins. So one of the principal functions of financial management is to provide the correct amount of working capital at the right time and in the right place to realise the greatest return on investment.

Working capital can initially be broken down into two types: permanent and temporary. Permanent working capital is tied up in keeping the business flowing throughout the year, while temporary working capital is needed from time to time to take account of seasonal, cyclical or unexpected fluctuations in the business. The latter type is usually serviced from an overdraft facility.

Both types of working capital have three major applications: firstly *inventories*, secondly *debtors* and finally *cash*.

Inventories can be further divided into inventories of raw materials, work in progress and finished goods. These three can soak up an enormous amount of excess working capital if not well managed. It is the job of the financial manager to minimise the stocks of raw materials, the level of the work in progress and the quantity of finished goods. However, over-stringent control can lead to disruption in production

Over-stringent cost control

Loss of sales

Disruption in production

Loss of customer goodwill

Failure to meet customer orders

caused by the delay in receiving raw materials, a failure to take account of costly price rises in the pipeline, a failure to keep the production volume required by future sales, and resulting expensive and damaging effects on customer goodwill. As one can see from the foregoing diagram, this can become a vicious circle where the loss of goodwill finally leads to loss of sales and results once again in stringent cost controls.

The just-in-time philosophy, developed in Japan, is aimed at reconciling these often conflicting interests and keeping inventory costs to a minimum.

On the debtor side, working capital is required to finance the gap between payment due to suppliers and payment owed by customers. It is the task of financial management to see that generous credit terms are negotiated with suppliers but minimal credit is offered to customers. Again a balance must be achieved between getting and giving good credit terms in order to attract customers and maintain positive relationships with suppliers on the one hand, and minimising cash outlay on the other hand.

Finally, cash is needed for both normal and abnormal requirements. Sound cash management will ensure that adequate cash is always available for meeting the company's day-to-day debts and that there is also a small reserve on hand to meet contingencies.

Chart 2.2

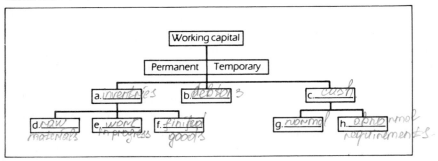

3 Comprehension/interpretation

3.1 For what purpose is temporary working capital required?

3.2 What methods are there to reduce the working capital required to finance debtors?

4 Language focus

4.1 Describing structures and systems (see Unit 69 in *Language Reference for Business English*)

Look at the following sentences taken from the Reading passage:

'Working capital *can initially be broken down into* two types . . .'
'The *latter type* is usually serviced from an overdraft facility.'

Now complete the passage which describes the organigram shown in Chart 2.3.

Chart 2.3

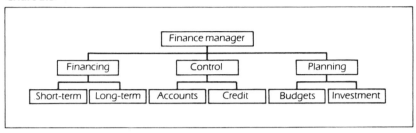

The finance department 1. _____ into three sections: financing, control and planning. Financing is further 2. _____ into short-term and long-term financing. The 3. _____ deals with the management of cash and working capital; the 4. _____ with long-term loans and repayments. The control function is also 5. _____ two sections: accounts and credit.

The accounts section 6. _____ for bookkeeping and production of management accounts; the credit function 7. _____ after credit terms and creditworthiness of suppliers. 8. _____, the planning department is 9. _____ two sections: budgets and investment. The 10. _____ is 11. _____ for collating departmental annual budgets and updating and revising them on a monthly basis while the 12. _____ assesses the return and profitability of new investment projects.

4.2   Cause and effect (see Unit 77 in *Language Reference for Business English*)

Look at the following sentence taken from the Reading passage:

'Over-stringent control *can lead to* disruption in production *caused by* delay in receiving new materials . . .'

Now use the diagram in the Reading passage to put the following parts of sentences into the correct order:

which will cause costs to be controlled.
and the subsequent loss of customer goodwill.
This will inevitably mean a decline in sales
Over-stringent control can lead to disruption in production
This may, in turn, result in the failure to meet customer orders
due to delays in raw materials.

5 *Word study*

5.1 **Raise** versus **rise**. Study the difference between these two sentences:

(i) The company **raised** its prices.
(ii) Prices **rose**.

In (i) there is an active agent – the company; in (ii) there is no active agent.
  Decide which verb to use in the following sentences. Make sure you use the right tense!

1. The issue of new shares _____ an additional £50,000 worth of capital.
2. I wish my salary would _____.
3. The _____ in inflation will cause us to _____ prices.
4. When the share price _____, I _____ my stake in the company.

5.2 Match the words on the left with the best opposite on the right.

1. to tie up	a.	too lax
2. to soak up	b.	past
3. over-stringent	c.	an intersection
4. in the pipeline	d.	to use sparingly
5. a vicious circle	e.	a virtuous circle
6. to reconcile	f.	to free
7. a gap	g.	to conflict

6 *Transfer*

Present the types and uses of working capital. Give examples from your own experience.

Part 2: Presenting a cash flow forecast

1 *Warm-up*

1.1 How does a company calculate its needs for working capital?
1.2 How can a company improve its cash flow?

2 *Listening*

Listen to the presentation of a cash flow forecast. As you listen, fill in the missing figures in Chart 2.4.

Chart 2.4

CASH FLOW FORECAST

	June	July	Aug.	Sept.	Oct.	Nov.
Opening cash balance		−11,300	−22,100	−29,400	_____	_____
Capital introduction	30,000					
Sales		2,000	5,000	10,000	15,000	18,000
Total receipts	30,000	2,000	5,000	10,000	15,000	18,000
Wages	6,000	_____	_____	_____	_____	_____
Raw materials	_____	1,500	_____	_____	_____	_____
Production overhead	1,500	1,500	1,500	1,500	1,500	1,500
Administrative overhead	_____	_____	_____	_____	_____	_____
Selling and distrib.	1,800	1,800	1,800	1,800	1,800	1,800
Factory rent	_____					
Equipment and machinery	_____					
Drawings	_____	_____	_____	_____	_____	_____
Total payments	41,300	12,800	12,300	12,300	12,300	12,300
Movement in cash	−11,300	−10,800	−7,300	−2,300	+3,700	+5,700
Closing cash balance	**−11,300**	**−22,100**	**−29,400**	_____	**−28,000**	_____

3 Comprehension/interpretation

3.1 Why are there no sales receipts until the second month?
3.2 Are his forecasts for overheads over-optimistic?
3.3 Does he think the rent is too high?
3.4 Why has he decided not to lease equipment?

4 Language focus

4.1 Future reference – forecasting (see Units 8 and 9 in *Language Reference for Business English*)

Look at the following sentences taken from the Listening passage:

   'The sales *will not begin* to picture until the second month . . .'
   'After that, they *rise* quite rapidly to reach . . .'

Now choose between the following three forms to complete the dialogue below:

will + verb   (e.g. *will rise*)
present simple (e.g. *rises*)
going to + verb (e.g. *is going to rise*)

A: When _____ you (plan) to open the factory?
B: We _____ (reckon) it _____ (open) at the beginning of July.
A: In the meantime, _____ you (promote) your product?
B: No, we _____ (hope) to start selling in July.
A: So you _____ not (expect) any orders in July?
B: Probably not, we _____ (anticipate) orders _____ (come) in from August onwards.
A: What level of sales _____ you (forecast) for August?
B: Well, we _____ (project) sales of about £20,000.
A: That _____ (sound) very optimistic. _____ you (have) the figures to support that?
B: No, not on me. We _____ (inform) all prospective customers by direct mail and we _____ (be) confident of £20,000 sales, as an early result.
A: The effect of direct mail _____ (be) notoriously difficult to predict. _____ you (do) anything else?
B: Yes, we _____ (telephone) all major users in the industry and arrange appointments.

4.2   Scale of likelihood (see Unit 80 in *Language Reference for Business English*)

Look at the following sentences taken from the Listening passage:

'That *should* settle down to about £1,000 per month.'
'*Certainly* it *should* sustain production running at . . .'

Now complete the following sentences so that they express the level of likelihood indicated in brackets:

1. We _____ to achieve sales of more than £30,000. (improbable)
2. We _____ lease equipment but interest rates are very high. (possible)
3. We _____ not reduce costs below this level. (impossible)
4. There's a _____ chance we _____ need an overdraft of £32,000. (probable)
5. Sales are _____ to rise in the second half of the year. (probable)
6. I _____ only take a salary of £1,000 a month. (certain)
7. We _____ be ready to start production next month. (probable)
8. There _____ be some difficulties in production at the start. (possible)

5 Word study

Match up the verbs with a suitable preposition to form an expression:

Verb	Preposition	Object
To work		the figures.
To put		your own money.
To start	**out**	a business.
To buy	**on**	raw materials.
	in	
To settle	**into**	a low figure.
To set	**up**	.
	down	
To put effort	**off**	sales.
To be better	**at**	.
To take		the profits.
To manage		a low salary.

6 Transfer

Analyse the cash flow forecast (Chart 2.4). Discuss whether you would give this entrepreneur a bank overdraft.

UNIT 3
Financial measurements

Section A: The profit and loss account

Part 1: Reading a profit and loss account

1 Warm-up

1.1 Why should managers keep an eye on the profit and loss account?

1.2 Why are investors interested in the profit and loss account?

2 Reading

Read the following explanation of profit and loss (P&L) accounts. As you read it, complete the statement of accounts (Chart 3.1).

The profit and loss account, also known as the income statement, summarises the profitability of the company by balancing revenue against expenses.

Revenue (sometimes called turnover) represents any increase in the owner's equity resulting from the operation of the business. Expenses are costs incurred in connection with the earning of revenue.

In the P&L account below (Chart 3.1), the direct costs, or cost of sales of £30 million, are deducted from the turnover of £65 million to reach a gross profit of £35 million. The operating profit is reached by deducting other operating expenses, sometimes called fixed costs (in this case £15.5 million) to reach a figure of £19.5 million as an operating profit. On some statements, especially consolidated accounts, minority interests will be deducted from this sum. In this case, £5.4 million is due to the minority shareholders in the company's subsidiaries and associated companies.

The profit figure now reached (£14.1 million) is taxable at whatever rate of corporation tax is applicable. This company pays £1.8 million in tax to end up with £12.3 million in profit after tax. This year, an amount of £450,000 is set aside as an extraordinary item. This represents a sum contributed to a special disaster fund.

The £11.85 million can now be distributed between shareholders and retentions to the reserves. In this case there are a small number of preference shareholders who receive a fixed dividend of £50,000 in total; a further £300,000 is paid out as a dividend to the ordinary shareholders. The company retains earnings of £11.5 million. Of particular interest to investors is the earnings per share, which has risen from 25p last year to 31p this year.

Chart 3.1

CONSOLIDATED PROFIT AND LOSS ACCOUNT		
	Year ended 31 December	
	1991	1990
	£000	£000
	65,000	60,000
	(30,000)	(29,000)
	35,000	31,000
	(15,500)	(14,800)
	19,500	16,200
	(5,400)	(4,800)
	14,100	11,400
	(1,800)	(1,900)
	12,300	9,500
	(450)	—
	11,850	9,500
	(50)	(40)
	(300)	(190)
	11,500	9,280
	31p	25p

3 Comprehension/interpretation

3.1 Compare this year's with last year's results. What are the significant changes?

3.2 What type of expenses would be included under 'other operating expenses (fixed costs)'?

3.3 What type of cost can be included under 'extraordindary items'?

3.4 What is the difference between preference and ordinary shares?

3.5 Why is the earnings per share interesting to the investor?

4 Language focus

4.1 Defining and non-defining relative clauses (see Unit 39 in *Language Reference for Business English*)

Look at the following sentences taken from the Reading passage:

> The profit and loss account, *also known as the income statement*, summarises the profitability . . .'
>
> 'In this case there are a small number of preference shareholders *who receive a fixed dividend of £50,000 in total* . . .'

Now combine the following sentences:

1. The profit and loss statement makes depressing reading.
   You received it yesterday.
2. The bookkeeper made some terrible mistakes.
   We hired him last year.
3. The accounts were audited two months late.
   You will find the accounts attached.
4. The production manager underestimated the operating costs.
   We fired the production manager two days ago.
5. Profits have still not been distributed to the employees.
   Profits were well down on last year.

4.2 Passive versus active voice (see Units 21 and 22 in *Language Reference for Business English*)

Look at the following sentences taken from the Reading passage:

> 'The direct costs . . . *are deducted* from the turnover . . .'
>
> 'This company *pays* £1.8 million in tax . . .'

Now change the following sentences from active to passive voice or vice versa:

1. The profit and loss account summarises the profitability of the company.
2. This company pays £1.8 million in tax.
3. The preference shareholders received a fixed dividend of £50,000.
4. Earnings of £11.5 million are retained by the company.
5. The accountants calculate the taxable profit.

6. Considerable costs have been incurred by investing in property.
7. We will maximise our profits by deferring taxation.
8. Savings would have been made by reducing production capacity.

5 *Word study*

With some words, many forms can be generated. For example:

to profit   **a profit**   **profitability**   **profitable**
(to make a profit)

Generate other forms (where indicated) of the following verbs:

Verb	*Noun*	*Adjective*
to operate	_____	_____
to deduct	_____	_____
to tax	_____	_____
to apply	_____	_____
to contribute	_____	
to retain	_____	
to distribute	_____	

6 *Transfer*

Explain the profit and loss account shown in Chart 3.2. What sort of business do you think this is?

Chart 3.2

PROFIT AND LOSS ACCOUNT				
		1991		1990
Income				
Sales		550,000		470,000
Direct costs				
Fees	350,000		330,000	
Premises	20,000		18,000	
Resource materials	5,000		10,000	
		375,000		358,000
		175,000		112,000
Expenses				
Rent	20,000		15,000	
Rates	1,500		1,500	
Insurance	2,500		2,400	
Heat and light	1,400		900	
Telecoms	7,800		6,100	
Repairs and renewals	3,500		1,100	
Administration salaries	29,000		20,000	
Office supplies	11,000		6,000	
Publicity and advert.	25,000		14,000	
Legal and professional	1,100			
Bank charges and interest	4,500		1,100	
		107,300		68,100
		67,000		43,900
Depreciation				
Building improvements	1,100		900	
Computers	4,200		3,100	
Fixtures and fittings	3,100			
		8,400	2,900	6,900
Net profit for the year		**58,600**		**37,000**

Part 2: Profit and cash flow

1 Warm-up

How can a company be highly profitable but short of cash?

2 Listening

Listen to the extract from an internal meeting. Two managers (one finance, the other marketing) are discussing the company's cash flow problems. As you listen, complete Chart 3.3 by ticking the problems which Pete and Simon analyse as the causes of the cash flow problem:

Chart 3.3

Problems	Pete (finance)	Simon (marketing)
Credit terms		
Investment planning		
Under-capitalisation		
Over-trading		
Financial planning		

3 Comprehension/interpretation

3.1 What have they recently invested in?
3.2 Why has the depreciation figure been so low in the P&L account?
3.3 How have they managed to increase their margins so substantially?
3.4 What happened to the funds which were retained for tax?

4 Language focus

4.1 Opinion-giving (see Unit 75 in *Language Reference for Business English*)

Look at the following extracts taken from the Listening passage:

> '*In my opinion*, the fundamental problem is our deferred terms of payment . . .'
> '*I think* you're exaggerating . . .'

Now classify the following expressions as strong (S), neutral (N) or Weak (W).

1. In my opinion . . .
2. There are two sides to the argument . . .
3. I'm absolutely convinced . . .
4. I tend to think . . .
5. It's true that . . .
6. There's absolutely no doubt that . . .
7. We believe . . .
8. I'm inclined towards saying . . .
9. I'm sure you'll agree with me . . .
10. Don't you think we should . . .

4.2   Agreeing and disagreeing (see Unit 76 in *Language Reference for Business English*)

Look at the following extracts taken from the Listening passage:

'Yes, that's probably true but I feel . . .'
'I resent that . . . I think my department . . .'

Now match phrases of agreement with those of disagreement. Match them so that they carry a similar strength of feeling:

1. I agree	a. I'm inclined to disagree
2. I couldn't agree more	b. I see your point of view but . . .
3. I'm with you	c. I disagree
4. I tend to agree	d. Rubbish!
5. I can see what you mean	e. I don't go along with that
6. You're absolutely right	f. I disagree entirely
7. Exactly!	g. You've missed my point altogether
8. That's exactly my point	h. You're completely wrong

5 Word study

We use a lot of emotive and descriptive adjectives when we talk about problems. Below you will find a collection of adjectives. Classify them under the four headings. An example has been given in each case.

irrelevant   noticeable   underlying   significant
sudden   instant   superficial   tiny
massive   marked   huge   enormous

Depth of problem	*Size of problem*	*Importance of problem*	*Timing*
fundamental	substantial	insignificant	immediate
_____	_____	_____	_____
_____	_____	_____	_____
_____	_____	_____	_____
	_____	_____	
	_____	_____	

6 Transfer

Write a summary of the problems facing the above company. Make some recommendation to solve their problems.

Section B: The balance sheet

Part 1: Explaining the balance sheet

1 Warm-up

1.1   What does the balance sheet tell you about a company?
1.2   What are the problems of calculating real values from the balance sheet?

2 Reading

Read the following explanation of the balance sheet. As you read it, fill in the headings in the left-hand column of Chart 3.4.

> The balance sheet is a statement of what a company owns (its assets) and what it owes (its liabilities) at a particular time. It consists of three major sections: assets, liabilities and equity.
>
> These three sections are arranged differently from country to country. In the USA and many European countries, the assets appear on the left-hand side of the

page and the liabilities on the right. In England, the three sections mentioned above are arranged vertically.

In the balance sheet below (Chart 3.4), the fixed assets are broken down into intangibles (such as patents and goodwill, entered in the books at a value of £1.5 million) and tangible assets (such as freehold property, land and equipment, at a book value of £7.5 million).

The next heading is current assets and this is split into three: firstly stocks valued at £3.2 million, then debtors (in other words outstanding payment for goods sold) at £1.3 million, and thirdly cash at the bank, worth £350,000. The total of current assets is then reduced by the total of current liabilities, which in this case is £2.2 million and represents amounts owing to creditors, leaving a net figure of £2.65 million. Thus the total assets less the current liabilities amount to £11.65 million.

To reach the final balance this figure must be reduced by the sum of long-term liabilities such as loans and also any provisions. In this case £2.45 million is set aside for long-term loans and there is a £450,000 provision for deferred taxation. So this leaves a final balance of £8.75 million worth of net assets.

The net asset figure is represented by the final section of the balance sheet – capital and reserves. This company has a share capital of £6.5 million. This sum is topped up by a share premium account which represents the difference between the above issued share value and the actual price of the shares. In this case, the capital is further increased by £1.4 million. The company has also revalued its fixed assets to give them a more realistic market price so that the shareholders' equity increases by a further £1.15 million and an equivalent amount is charged to depreciation in the profit and loss account. Finally, £300,000 is deducted in retained profit.

Chart 3.4

	BALANCE SHEET			
as at 31 December		1991 £000		1990 £000
_____				
_____		1,500		1,400
_____		7,500		7,200
		9,000		8,600
_____				
_____	3,200		2,800	
_____	1,300		1,400	
_____	350		250	
	4,850		4,450	
_____				
_____	(2,200)		(2,100)	
_____		2,650		2,350
_____		11,650		10,950
_____		(2,450)		(2,850)
_____		(450)		
_____		8,750		8,100
_____				
_____		6,500		6,500
_____		1,400		1,200
_____		1,150		800
_____		(300)		(400)
Shareholders' funds		**8,750**		**8,100**

3 Comprehension/interpretation

3.1 In many companies, intangible fixed assets do not appear in the balance sheet. In what circumstances must a company value its intangible assets?

3.2 Why should taxation be deferred?

3.3 Why is it sometimes necessary to account for the share premium?

4 Language focus

4.1 Prepositions – amount and difference (see Unit 68 in *Language Reference for Business English*)

Look at the following sentences taken from the Reading passage:

'This figure must be reduced *by* the sum of the long-term liabilities . . .'
'This leaves a balance *of* £8.75 million . . .'

Now complete the sentences below with the correct prepositions:

1. When current liabilities are subtracted _____ current assets, there is a net balance _____ £50,000.
2. Debtors have increased _____ last year's figure of £25,000 _____ a total _____ £48,000.
3. Our bank loan has decreased _____ 10 per cent, so a balance _____ £25,000 remains.
4. The bank overdraft stood _____ £18,000 last year. It has been reduced _____ £5,000 and now stands _____ £13,000.
5. There has been an increase _____ 2 per cent per year in interest payments. So in fact it's rocketed _____ 6 per cent in 1987 _____ 12 per cent this year.

4.2 Sequence (see Unit 67 in *Language Reference for Business English*)

Look at the following extract from the Reading passage:

'The *next* heading is current assets . . .: *firstly* . . ., *then* . . . *and thirdly* . . .'

Now put the following process in the right order:

SETTING UP A JOINT VENTURE
a. If no published accounts are available, then you should check on its financial standing with credit agencies.
b. Initially, s/he may be wary of your approach.
c. In the meeting, you should identify clear objectives for both sides.
d. The first step is to identify a company in the right sector.
e. Once you have a clear picture of its financial status, arrange to meet the managing director.
f. Finally, it's important to remember that however good the relationship, a clear legal contract is necessary to cement the deal.
g. Having done this, you need to look closely at its published accounts.
h. However, once you have made your intentions clear, you should be able to establish a good relationship.

5 Word study

Item	Value expression	Amount
Property	is valued at has been revalued at amounts to is worth is set at a book value of is topped up by	£25 million

Amount	Value expression	Item
£25 million	is charged to is entered under is set aside for	fixed assets

Now complete these sentences:

1. The land _____ at $40 million.
2. $40 million _____ for the land.
3. The share value was too low so it _____ by £10 million.
4. Fixed assets _____ of £20 million. However, in reality they _____ at least £35 million.
5. An additional $400,000 _____ to depreciation.

6 Transfer

Now explain the following balance sheet. What sort of business do you think it is?

Chart 3.5

BALANCE SHEET				
As at 1 April		1991		1990
Fixed assets				
Freehold property		350,000		350,000
Computer equipment		80,000		40,000
Fixtures and fittings		75,000		45,000
		505,000		435,000
Current assets				
Debtors	89,000		75,000	
Stock	58,000		50,000	
	147,000		125,000	
Current liabilities				
Bank overdraft	25,000		18,000	
Creditors	25,000		22,000	
	50,000		40,000	
Net current assets		**97,000**		**85,000**
Total assets *less* current liabilities		602,000		520,000
Long-term creditors				
Secured liability on property		290,000		300,000
Accrued interest payable		56,000		68,000
Bank loan		80,000		20,000
Net assets		**176,000**		**132,000**
Represented by:				
Partners' capital accounts	120,000		110,000	
Partners' current accounts	56,000		22,000	
		176,000		132,000

Part 2: Valuing goodwill

1 Warm-up

1.1   What does the goodwill of a company really represent?
1.2   How can the goodwill value be calculated?

2 Listening

Listen to the extract from a meeting to discuss the valuation of the company. As you listen, complete Chart 3.6.

Chart 3.6

Assets	Net asset value	Long-term liabilities		Target price
Earnings (goodwill)	Average profits	Average turnover	Gross margin	Target price

3 Comprehension/interpretation

3.1   Why are Technics interested in this firm?
3.2   Why won't they be interested in the assets?
3.3   What will the current net asset value cover?
3.4   Are the firm's net profits outstanding?

4 Language focus

4.1   Continuous verb forms (see Units 1, 4 and 6 in *Language Reference for Business English*)

Look at the following extracts taken from the Listening passage:

> 'Technics *will be looking* for a good return on their capital . . .'
> 'We *should be looking* for a goodwill figure of about £500,000 . . .'

Now decide whether you can use a continuous form of the verbs in *italic* to stress the ongoing nature of an event in the following sentences. Where it is possible, change the verb.

1. We *will make* a profit of $100,000 this year.
2. We *should invest* in time share deals.
3. They *have reported* a £20 million loss.
4. They *have lost* money continuously.
5. We *invested* £10 million in the project and we *lost* it all.

6. We *recruited* salesmen throughout the year.
7. He always *talks* about things; he never *does* them.
8. We *attract* offers regularly.
9. She *has acquired* two companies recently.
10. He *has acquired* companies all his life.

4.2 Verb + preposition: **to look** . . . (see Unit 31 in *Language Reference for Business English*)

Look at the following sentence taken from the Listening passage:

'Technics will be *looking for* a good return on their capital . . .'

Now complete the following sentences with an appropriate preposition:

1. If you look _____ your current figures, they don't make happy reading.
2. We've taken on a consultant. She's going to look _____ our supply chain.
3. You shouldn't look _____ to consultants. They make mistakes like the rest of us.
4. We've been looking _____ a new bookkeeper for weeks; maybe we need to advertise nationally.
5. I looked _____ the telephone number in the directory.
6. Finance managers should never look _____ on other departmental managers, just because they don't understand finance.
7. We're looking _____ the possibility of subcontracting some of the production. It looks _____ if it may be possible.
8. If you look _____ the pennies, the pounds will take care of themselves.

5 *Word study*

Talking about figures. Study how we can be more or less precise when we discuss figures:

just over/above a bit more than	200,000+	
precisely exactly	200,000	about around in the region of approximately
just under/below nearly almost	200,000−	

Listen to the cassette. You will hear a number of figures. Round them up or down and use one of the above phrases. For example:

199,400 → around 200,000
                just under 200,000

6 *Transfer*

Present the analysis of the valuation using Chart 3.6 above.

UNIT 4
Financial analysis

Section A: Ratio analysis

Part 1: Ratio analysis

1 *Warm-up*

1.1 If you're looking for a general picture of the financial state of a company, what figures would interest you most?

1.2 Investors, employees, managers and customers are interested in different aspects of a company's financial condition. What figures would these four parties be most interested in?

2 *Reading*

Read the following text about financial ratios and complete Chart 4.1 below.

There are four critical areas of a company's business which can be analysed by applying ratios. These are *liquidity, capital structure, activity and efficiency*, and *profitability*.

Measurements of liquidity should answer the question: Can a company pay its short-term debts? There are two ratios commonly used to answer this question. Firstly, the *current ratio*, which measures the current assets against the current liabilities. In most cases, a healthy company would show a ratio above 1, in other words more current assets than current liabilities. Another method of measuring liquidity is the so-called *quick ratio* – this is particularly appropriate in manufacturing industries where stock levels can disguise the company's true liquidity. The ratio is calculated in the same way as above but the stocks are deducted from the current assets.

The balance sheet will also reveal the gearing of the company – this is an indicator of the company's capital structure and its ability to meet its long-term debts. The ratio expresses the relationship between shareholders' funds and loan capital. Income gearing is also important and shows the ratio between profit and interest paid on borrowings. Relatively high borrowings would indicate vulnerability to an interest rate rise. Highly geared companies generally represent a greater risk for investors.

The balance sheet and the profit and loss account can be used to assess how efficiently a company manages its assets. Basically, sales are compared with investment in various assets. For example, in the retail sector, an important ratio which indicates efficiency is sales divided by stock – the resulting figure should be much higher than in the manufacturing sector where stock tends to show a much slower turnover. Another example of efficiency measurement is to calculate the average collection period on debts. This is found by dividing debtors by the sales per day. This can vary tremendously from industry to industry. In the retail sector it may well be as low as one or two days, whereas in the heavy manufacturing and service sectors it can range from thirty to ninety days.

Finally, profitability ratios show the manager's use of the company's resources. The profit margin figure (profit before tax divided by sales and expressed as a percentage) indicates the operational day-to-day profitability of the business. Return on capital employed can be calculated in a number of ways. One common method is to take profit before taxes and divide by the total assets – this is a good indicator of the use of all the assets of the company. From a shareholder's point of view, the return on owner's equity will be an important ratio; this is calculated by dividing the profit before taxes by the owner's equity and expressing it as a percentage. If the company does not earn a reasonable return, the share price will fall and thus make it difficult to attract additional capital.

Chart 4.1

Key indicators	Ratios used	Interpretation
Liquidity	(i) ———————	—————————————————
	(ii) ———————	—————————————————
Capital structure	(i) ———————	—————————————————
	(ii) ———————	—————————————————
Efficiency	(i) ———————	—————————————————
	(ii) ———————	—————————————————
Profitability	(i) ———————	—————————————————
	(ii) ———————	—————————————————
	(iii) ———————	—————————————————

3 Comprehension/interpretation

Which of the ratios is likely to be the key indicator for the following groups?

3.1 Shareholders
3.2 Managers
3.3 Customers
3.4 Suppliers
3.5 Employees

4 Language focus

4.1 Adjective modification (see Unit 49 in *Language Reference for Business English*)

Look at the following sentences taken from the Reading passage:

'This is *particularly appropriate* in manufacturing industries where stock levels . . .'
'*Relatively high* borrowing would indicate vulnerability to an interest rate rise.'

Now combine two adjectives from the list below to complete the sentences:

high	long	short	high	dangerous
particular	lower	unusual	geared	considerable

1. Normally a healthy company has a current ratio above 1. This company has an _____ _____ ratio of 2.
2. _____ _____ companies generally represent a greater risk for investors.
3. Retail companies have _____ _____ collection periods on debts.
4. Most people would consider a collection period over 90 days as _____ _____.
5. Manufacturing companies have a _____ _____ stock turnover than retail companies.

4.2 Adjectives and adverbs (see Unit 48 in *Language Reference for Business English*)

Look at the following sentences taken from the Reading passage:

The balance sheet and the profit and loss account can be used to assess how *efficiently* a company manages it assets.'
'Finally, *profitability* ratios show the managers' use of the company's resources.'

Now complete the list below:

Noun	Adjective	Adverb
profitability	profitable	_____
efficiency	_____	_____
health	_____	_____
appropriacy	_____	_____
operation	_____	_____
finance	_____	_____
productivity	_____	_____
management	_____	_____

5 Word study

5.1 Group the following adjectives under the headings indicated.

healthy	reasonable	disastrous	disappointing	excellent
satisfactory	vulnerable	poor	adequate	weak
marvellous	moderate	strong	tremendous	catastrophic

Positive	Average/okay	Negative
_____	_____	_____
_____	_____	_____
_____	_____	_____
_____	_____	_____
_____		_____
		_____

5.2 Now study how we can use these adjectives? For example:

we can say: *The company is in a vulnerable position.*
we cannot say: *The company had vulnerable results.*

Which of the adjectives in 5.1 above *cannot* be used with the following nouns:

1. _____ results
2. _____ condition/position

6 Transfer

Study the P&L account and the balance sheet (Charts 3.2 and 3.5 in Unit 3). Use the ratios in Chart 4.1 to analyse its current financial state (make comparisons with the previous year's figures).

Part 2: Business analysis

1 Warm-up

Besides the above ratios, what other business data would you like to have in order to judge the performance of a company?

2 Listening

Listen to an internal meeting between a finance manager and head of marketing. As you listen, complete Chart 4.2.

Chart 4.2

Sectors of business	Market share (%)	Market growth	Turnover (%)	Profits (%)	Investment (%)

3 Comprehension/interpretation

Do you think the marketing manager is turnover-oriented or profit-oriented?

4 Language focus

4.1 Present continuous (see Unit 1 in *Language Reference for Business English*)

Look at the following sentences taken from the Listening passage:

'We'*re operating* in three major sectors of consultancy work . . .'
'These three sectors *are growing* at different rates . . .'

Now decide if the verbs in *italic* in the sentences below need to be changed to the present continuous. If so, change them:

1. We currently *hold* about 10 per cent of the financial consultancy market.
2. The human resource sector *expands* rapidly at the moment.
3. He always *works* too hard.
4. We *gain* market share in the present climate.
5. If this recession continues, we *will lose* our position.
6. What *does* he *do*? He *telephones* America.
7. I *feel* we should withdraw from the market.
8. I *wait* for the results of the survey. Then I *will decide*.

4.2   Presentation – linkers (see Skill 1 in *Language Reference for Business English*)

Look at the following extracts from the Listening passage:

> '*So let me start by* reviewing where we stand.'
> '*I was just coming to that. Before I do, let me just add . . .*'

Now match the phrases with the functions for structuring a presentation:

Function	*Phrases*
1. Introducing the topic	a. Let me start by
2. Giving an outline	b. I'll come to that later
3. Starting a point	c. Incidentally, you may be interested
4.	to know
Finishing a point	d. Well, thank you for your attention: I'm
5.	sure you've got some questions
6. Moving on to another point	e. I've divided my talk into three parts
7. Referring backwards	f. That's all I have to say about
8. Referring forwards	g. As I mentioned earlier
9. Digressing	h. Let me just add
10. Adding information	i. Let's move on now to the question of
Closing the talk	j. Today, I'd like to talk about

5   *Word study*

Match the words/expressions on the left with the best synonym on the right:

1. views	a. to forecast
2. to review	b. to give to
3. to estimate	c. to assign
4. to move into a market	d. to hold market share
5. to build on your strength	e. to grow
6. static	f. opinions
7. to expand	g. to summarise
8. to be in line with	h. to be compatible with
9. to contribute to	i. to take advantage of your strong points
10. to fit in with	j. stable
11. to allocate	k. to be as expected/budgeted
12. to maintain market share	l. to enter a market

6 *Transfer*

DISCUSSION
Which are the most important constraints and opportunities for a company?

- Financial constraints/opportunities
- Marketing constraints/opportunities
- Personnel constraints/opportunities
- Others

Section B: Financial evaluation

Part 1: Capital investment budgeting

1 *Warm-up*

How can the accountant or financial manager take account of variables such as fluctuating interest rates when assessing the viability of a capital investment project?

2 *Reading*

Read the chief accountant's report. As you read it, complete Chart 4.3.

FINANCIAL EVALUATION
Project: Automation of No. 3 assembly line
Estimated cost: $2,000,000 (see detailed costing attached)

Introduction
This project has been very carefully costed and all the production, quality and short-term financial benefits are undisputed. This short report aims to evaluate the return on investment over a full five year period.

Findings
If we adopt a simple payback method of analysis, the project will recoup its investment after three years. However, it is vital that we take a more complex view of the project given that there are other competing projects involving similar sums. It is important that we look at the return and cash flow implications over a full five years and take account of the opportunity cost of this investment.

If we adopt an average rate of return (ARR) method, we can spread the cash flow beyond the payback period to the full five years and we calculate an ARR of 40%. This figure would seem to be considerably better than some competing projects.

However, this method does not take account of the time-value of money and therefore can give a very misleading rate of return. We have therefore applied a discounted cash flow calculation which translates any future earnings into their present-day value. In the table below, we have set the discounted cash flow at two different rates: firstly 10% which is 2% above the current bank base rate, and secondly 25% which is 2% above the best rate of return we earn from one of the franchise operations in our portfolio.

It is clear that at 10% DCF the project shows a very healthy profitability of $932,000 net after five years' operation; at 25% DCF the project breaks even in the fifth year.

Conclusion

The 25% DCF makes the project look very unattractive but, as stated above, this is based on a highly competitive, if not unrealistic rate of return. The true picture lies somewhere in between. This means we can probably expect an internal rate of return of about 15% on this project.

Recommendation

Given the activities of our competitors and the increasing difficulty of employing skilled workers to run our existing semi-automated production line, I would recommend the project is adopted.

Chief Accountant

Chart 4.3

	Capital cost	year 1	year 2	year 3	year 4	year 5
10% DCF	−2,000	546	496	600	546	744
Cumulative cash flow	−2,000	−1,454	−958	−358	188	a. _____
25% DCF	−2,000	−480	384	410	330	396
Cumulative cash flow	−2,000	−1,520	−1,136	−726	−396	b. _____

3 Comprehension/interpretation

What are the advantages/disadvantages of the three methods mentioned?

3.1 Straightforward payback method
3.2 Average rate of return
3.3 Discounted cash flow

4 Language focus

4.1 Conditions (see Unit 10 in *Language Reference for Business English*)

Look at the following sentence taken from the Reading section:

> '*If* we *adopt* a simple payback method of analysis, the project *will recoup* its investment after three years.'

Now complete the following sentences by putting the verbs in the right form:

1. If the project _____ (fail), we _____ (lose) a lot of money.
2. We _____ (can) extend the payback period if we _____ (adopt) an ARR method.
3. We _____ (get) a truer picture if we _____ (take) into account present values of money.
4. We _____ not (invest) unless we _____ (foresee) a realistic chance of long-term profits.
5. As long as the project _____ (be financed) from outside sources, we _____ (have to) ensure a much higher rate of return.
6. If we _____ (lose) money in the first two years, we _____ (start) to doubt the viability of the project.
7. Unless we _____ (be committed) to the project long-term, we _____ not (carry) it through.
8. Breakeven point _____ (come) a year earlier if we _____ (manage) to reach these sales targets.

4.2 Report-writing (see Skill 5 in *Language Reference for Business English*)

Look at the following sentences taken from the Reading passage:

> '*This short report aims* to evaluate the return on investment. . . .'
> 'Given the activities of our competitors . . . *I would recommend* the project is adopted.'

One of the decisions a report writer must make is whether to use a *personal* or *impersonal* style. Now change the following from personal to impersonal (avoid the use of *I/we*):

1. In this report, I aim to evaluate the return on investment . . .
2. It is vital that we take a more complex view of the project.
3. If we adopt the ARR method, we can spread the cash flow.
4. We have therefore applied a DCF method.
5. We have set the DCF at two different rates.
6. This means we can probably expect an internal rate of return of about 18%.
7. We can conclude that the 25% DCF is unrealistic.
8. Given the activities of our competitors, I would recommend the project is adopted.

5 Word study

Match the financial terms on the left with a situation on the right:

Financial terms	Situations
1. Opportunity cost	a. The company is putting together a number of shareholdings in a variety of companies
2. Time-value of money	b. The company must consider what else it could do with its money
3. Investment portfolio	c. We must calculate the benefit to the company not only in terms of the market's calculations.
4. Breakeven point	d. The company must take into account the project's value in present-day figures
5. Internal rate of return	e. The least we can achieve is for sales to cover our costs

6 Transfer

Use the report above as a basis to explain capital investment budgeting. Apply it to an example from your own experience.

Part 2: Costing and pricing a new product

1 Warm up

How does a company decide on an appropriate price for a new product?

2 Listening

Listen to an extract from a meeting in which the costing and pricing of a new product are discussed. As you listen, complete the cost/price breakdown in Chart 4.4

Chart 4.4

Recommended retail price

	a. _____
Discount	
	b. _____
Retailer's margin	
	c. _____
Manufacturer's margin	
	d. _____
Fixed costs	
	e. _____
Direct costs	

3 Comprehension/interpretation

3.1 What is the difference between direct (variable) costs and fixed (overhead) costs?

3.2 What sorts of mark-up would you expect in the following sectors: food, consumer durables (e.g. televisions), and services (e.g. consultancy, training)?

3.3 Why does a drop in production mean an increase in total cost per unit?

3.4 What is the advantage of setting a discounted retail price?

4 Language focus

4.1 Conditionals I and II (see Unit 10 in *Language Reference for Business English*)

Look at the following sentences taken from the Listening passage:

'What *if we achieve* higher sales through a lower retail price?'
'*If we lost* sales through too high a price, it *would jeapordise* the whole project.'

Now complete the following sentences:

1. If we _____ (set) a market price of £13, what _____ that (do) to sales?
2. We _____ still (protect) our margins if we fixed a price of £11.50.
3. If the market could bear it, we _____ (able to) push the price up.
4. We would lose market share if our competitor _____ (drop) its price.
5. I _____ (resign) if I _____ (win) the lottery.
6. Unless there is a price war, we _____ (make) a good profit.
7. If production _____ (fall), our unit costs will go up.
8. We _____ not (offer) a discount if the retailers are prepared to limit their margins.

4.2 Verb + preposition (see Units 31 and 32 in *Language Reference for Business English*)

Look at the following sentences taken from the Listening passage:

'So can we all *agree about* the facts?'
'That's a fair average *based on* projected sales figures . . .'

Now complete the following sentences by inserting one of the prepositions below:

on   up   at   to   from   out   with   for   down

1. We compared our prices _____ our competitors'.
2. Do you agree _____ Peter?
3. They agreed _____ the project and signed the contract.
4. These figures have been worked _____ by our accountants.
5. Sales are likely to respond quickly _____ changes in price.
6. If we push _____ the price, sales might come _____.
7. Are you prepared _____ the price war?
8. We aimed _____ a lower price than out competitors.
9. We set the price _____ £12.50.
10. We prevented the competitors _____ gaining market share.

5 Word study

Match the expressions on the left with their best equivalents on the right:

1. projected	a. shop
2. achieve	b. perceived value
3. mark-up	c. cautious
4. retail outlet	d. endanger
5. elastic	f. forecast
6. set (a price)	g. increase
7. jeopardise	h. reach
8. conservative	i. responsive to price
9. push up (the price)	j. margin
10. price the market can bear	k. fix

6 Transfer

Write a brief report about the pricing of the above product. Use these headings.

- Introduction
- Findings
- Conclusions
- Recommendations

UNIT 5
Standards and compliance

Section A: Standardising financial reporting on a European basis

Part 1: Comparability of accounts

1 Warm-up

1.1 What are the audiences that companies aim at when they publish their financial accounts?

1.2 When judging a company's position/value, what are the key figures?

2 Reading

Read the following article 'Flying in the face of accounting convention' by Richard Waters. As you read it, complete the Chart 5.1.

Comparing the results of companies in different countries is like comparing apples with pears, and not just because they report in different currencies.

National accounting systems have developed at different rates and under different pressures (shareholder pressure in the Anglo-Saxon world, government pressure in many continental European countries). Net income reported under one convention bears little resemblance to that reported under another.

Does it matter? A growing number of accountants, stock exchanges and regulators think that it does. International capital markets cannot work efficiently without full information about the companies that are competing for capital. The debt markets have survived on credit ratings produced by recognised agencies: but equity investors, who are concerned with more than security and a fixed rate of return, need other, better ways of comparing companies.

The International Accounting Standards Committee, at its quarterly meeting in Copenhagen this month, took an important step in trying to tighten up international accounting rules. With the backing of stock exchanges, it hopes that these can become the standard for companies raising capital outside their home countries.

It is now up to companies, investors and regulators to decide whether the IASC's ideas should be taken forward. Lest they underestimate the importance of the task, they should consider the following example.

Airlines are big business. They have also sold a lot of shares to the public in recent years as governments around the world have shed their stakes in their national carriers. However, it is virtually impossible to compare the performance of different national airlines.

Take Japan Air Lines, which reported a net loss of $28m (£15.27m) in the year to March 31 1987 (to make comparisons easier, all figures have been translated into US dollars, either at exchange rates given by the company, such as JAL, or at the rate prevailing at the year end in question). Before understanding JAL's results a reader needs to consider the following items:

- Japanese tax law allows companies to delay reporting income arising from insurance claims. JAL's delayed income from this source amounted to $76m during 1987 – nearly three times its reported profits.
- JAL set aside $65m during the year to cover the expected costs of severance pay, but says that is only 40 per cent of the full amount. This implies that the full deduction from profits should have been $162.5m, although JAL gives no explanation in its accounts for this huge amount. The 40 per cent is tax-deductible, suggesting that the provision was made simply to take advantage of this tax concession.
- The discount on bonds issued during the year was written off to profits. Elsewhere in the world, a consensus is forming that such costs are part of a company's financing cost and should be spread over a number of years. The effect of JAL's method: $7m off profits.

JAL is not alone in posing difficult questions for anyone hoping to arrive at its true profits. British Airways, which last year took over British Caledonian, adopted the standard British way of accounting for its acquisition: it wrote off the goodwill of £663m against reserves.

A US airline would have been required to write it off against future profits, although it could spread the cost over 40 years. When a new Australian accounting rule is introduced, an airline in that country would have to spread the cost over no more than 20 years.

Ignoring for a moment the rights or wrongs of these different approaches, the fact remains that they produce very different results. The IASC's proposal is for goodwill to be written off over five years. That is bound to arouse antagonism on all sides, presenting the IASC with the difficult task of convincing companies that comparability should come before their national version of what is right.

However, it is possible to compare BA to other countries' airlines, or at least those listed in the US. BA has to translate its figures into US accounting language as a condition of being listed there. The result: British profits of $285m become US net income of $350m.

The industry, needless to say, does not rely on such unreliable figures for making performance comparisons. Its performance measure is revenue tonne kilometres – the number of miles of air travel that an airline sells during a year. This is the same in any language and does not need translating.

The difficulty of comparing profits shrinks into insignificance when compared with the difficulties of comparing balance sheets and, by extension, key ratios like gearing, return on capital, and so on.

A glance at the value of airline fleets shown in different companies' accounts points to one fundamental difficulty. Lufthansa operates 151 aircraft which are shown in its accounts at nearly $3bn. JAL's 77 aircraft (half the size of Lufthansa's fleet), on the other hand, are recorded at $6.6bn, or more than twice the amount. And what about KLM's 79 aircraft at $2bn and BA's 197 at $3.3bn? The different mix of aircraft operated by different airlines, or different age profiles, surely does not account for such differences.

The first difficulty is that there are different methods of valuation. Whereas Lufthansa is required by law to show assets at historical cost, for instance, BA appears to feel free to apply various valuation methods to its aircraft. A revaluation of most of them in 1987 led to an additional $520m – equivalent to nearly half of BA's total shareholders' funds.

However, it did not revalue Concorde, which according to the accounts has a value of precisely nothing. With a range of valuation methods between different companies, not to mention different rates of depreciation, it becomes impossible to compare the value of fleets.

The second difficulty is that some aircraft are not shown in the balance sheet at all. Leased aircraft either may or may not be included, depending on the type of lease. Different countries have different tests for determining what should be recorded, making it still more difficult to compare airlines.

As a general rule, the more aircraft that do not appear in the balance sheet, the greater the level of borrowings that are kept out of the accounts and the lower the company's gearing. Airlines may argue persuasively that they should not have to bring all leased assets on to their accounts, but this does not make the readers' task any easier.

Aircraft valuation becomes a simple exercise when compared with other balance-sheet problems. Take the UK and US versions of BA's balance sheet. UK rules give the company shareholders' funds of $1.2bn.

US accounting, on the other hand, adds $680m to this to reflect the value of goodwill that has been written off in the UK accounts; knocks off $575m to bring BA's fleet back to its historical cost; and takes away a further $233m to reflect the extra deferred taxes that US accounting rules say should be provided for.

These are all big numbers. But which version is 'right'? At least the figures are available to allow the informed reader to make up his or her own mind. For many other companies they are not. And even when they are, it would be better if it were not left to the reader to make the adjustments.

The IASC is trying to fill this gap. However, it has a tough job ahead of it if it is to persuade the world that its rules are the right ones.

Chart 5.1

Airline	Profit/loss	Value of fleet (no. of aircraft)
JAL	a. _____	c. _____
BA	b. _____	d. _____
Lufthansa	–	e. _____
KLM	–	f. _____

3 Comprehension/interpretation

3.1 Why does it matter that national accounting systems differ?
3.2 What additional income did JAL not report in their 86/87 figures?
3.3 What additional costs did JAL not report?
3.4 In what other way did JAL reduce their profits?
3.5 What measure does the industry use for comparing airline company performance?
3.6 What are the two main reasons why valuations of fleets vary from country to country?
3.7 Why do the UK and US valuations of shareholders' funds in BA's balance sheet differ so much?

4 Language focus

4.1 Connectors (see Units 67 and 72 in *Language Reference for Business English*)

Look at the following sentences taken from the Reading passage:

'A US airline would have been required to write it off against future profits, *although* it could spread the cost over 40 years.'
'*Whereas* Lufthansa is required by law to show assets at historical cost, BA appears to feel free to apply various valuation methods . . .'

Now use the following connectors to combine the sentences:

although   whereas   however   even though   despite

1. _____ having to set aside $20m for redundancies, the company showed a profit.
2. _____ the company showed a profit, the balance sheet looks increasingly fragile.
3. American companies must add goodwill values to shareholders' funds _____ British companies can simply write them off.
4. We made an overall loss _____ our American operations were highly profitable.
5. The industry has its own methods of analysing performance. _____, analysts need to be able to evaluate comparable accounts.

4.2   Subordinate clauses (see Unit 36 in *Language Reference for Business English*)

Look at the following sentence taken from the Reading passage:

'The debt markets have survived on credit ratings *produced by recognised agencies*: but equity investors, *who are concerned with more than security and a fixed rate of return*, need other, better ways of comparing companies.'

Now expand the following subordinate clauses in italics. The first one has been done for you.

1. Japanese tax laws allow companies to delay reporting income *arising from insurance claims*.
   → which arises from insurance claims.
2. The 40 per cent is tax deductible, *suggesting that the provision was made simply to take advantage of this tax concession*.
3. The discount on bonds *issued during the year* was written off to profits.
4. JAL is not alone in posing difficult questions for anyone *hoping to arrive at its true profits*.
5. That is bound to arouse antagonism on all sides, *presenting the IASC with the difficult task* . . .
6. A glance at the value of airline fleets *shown in different company accounts* points to one fundamental difficulty . . .
7. The different mix of aircraft *operated by different airlines* surely does not account for such difficulties.
8. Different countries have different tests for determining what should be recorded, *making it still more difficult to compare airlines*.

5 Word study

Choose the appropriate preposition from the middle column to complete the expression:

to tighten		standards
to arise		insurance claims
to amount	for	$20 million
to set	away	$60m for taxation
to take advantage	off	a tax concession
to write	up	a bad debt
to spread	over	ten years
to translate	into	dollars
to be recorded	from	$20 million
to account	out	depreciation
to apply	aside	cost calculations
to keep	to	of the accounts
to bring	of	the accounts
to knock	at	the value
to take		from the profits

6 Transfer

Take the annual reports of two or three major companies in one sector (e.g. electronics, energy, etc.). Study the key income and balance sheet figures. Are they comparable? What special conditions/concessions apply (study the notes to the accounts)?

Part 2: Analysing performance

1 Warm-up

1.1   What are the problems of analysing companies from their annual reports?
1.2   How can you judge future performance from past results?

2 Listening

Listen to the extract from a meeting in which two companies are being compared. As you listen, complete Chart 5.2.

Chart 5.2

	Saxon	Pixbury
Development costs		
Bond issue		
Net income		
Assets: equity		
intangibles		

3   Comprehension/interpretation

3.1   How do you think R&D costs should be accounted for in the P&L account and balance sheet?

3.2   How do you think goodwill should be accounted for when acquiring a company?

4   Language focus

4.1   Meetings – introductions and controlling (see Skill 2 in *Language Reference for Business English*)

Look at the following extracts from the Listening passage:

'Okay gentlemen, let's get started.'
'So, John, would you like to put us in the picture?'

Now match the expression with its function in a meeting.

Function	Expression

Function

1. Opening the meeting
2. Agreeing the agenda
3. Introducing the first item
4. Asking for contributions
5. Paraphrasing/clarifying
6. Asking for further contributions
7. Allowing somebody to finish
8. Stopping someone talking
9. Summarising
10. Closing the meeting

Expression

a.   Peter, would you like to start the ball rolling?
b.   Just a moment. Let John finish.
c.   Let me just recap then. What we've agreed is . . .
d.   Okay, let's get down to business.
e.   If I understand you correctly, you're saying . . .
f.   Michael, that's interesting. Let's hear from somebody else.
g.   Has anybody anything further to add?
h.   Has everybody seen the agenda? All happy with it?
i.   So, let's call it a day.
j.   Let's move straight away to the first item.

4.2 Degree – modification of adjectives (see Unit 49 in *Language Reference for Business English*)

Look at the following sentences taken from the Listening passage:

'On the face of it, Saxon performed *much* better than Pixbury last year.'
'Pixbury have a *much* more modest figure . . .'

Now classify the following adverbs of degree as strong (S), neutral (N) or weak (W).

1. considerably
2. somewhat
3. slightly
4. quite a lot
5. a lot

6. moderately
7. a little
8. much
9. marginally
10. significantly

5 *Word study*

Group these words under the four headings given below:

dynamic	state-of-the-art	substantial	low-key ·	enterprising
modest	conservative	go-ahead	high-tech	cautious
healthy	leading edge	advanced	strong	modern
thrusting	robust			

Forward-looking companies	*Technology*	*Asset base*	*Reporting policy*
——————	——————	——————	——————
——————	——————	——————	——————
——————	——————	——————	——————
——————	——————	——————	——————
	——————		

6 *Transfer*

Pick two more companies in one sector. Use their past results (annual reports) to analyse potential future performance.

Section B: The role of auditors

Part 1: The role of auditors

1 *Warm-up*

1.1 What are the main responsibilities of an auditor?
1.2 Do you think business fraud is widespread?

2 Reading

Read the article 'Auditors may assume the role of whistle-blower' by David Walker. After you have read it, complete the true/false exercise.

An auditor finds out early in his training that he is a watchdog and not a bloodhound. From today, when the Auditing Practices Committee (APC) issues its long-awaited guideline on auditors and fraud, an auditor will also have to consider himself a whistle-blower.

The guideline, which follows a gestation period of no less than five years, sets out to clarify auditors' responsibilities in relation to fraud, as well as other irregularities and errors. It recommends that auditors take a modestly pro-active role in reporting fraud to third parties.

The document acknowledges that an auditor's primary duty is one of confidentiality to the client. But the document says an auditor should also consider throwing this narrow duty aside and think of the wider public interest.

Taking its cue from an ethical statement issued in 1988, Professional Contact in Relation to Defaults or Unlawful Acts, the document spells out the circumstances when the public interest could be served by a nod and a wink to the Department of Trade and Industry or some other official authority.

Under normal circumstances, the auditor's first step would be to alert the client's management to the existence of fraud. But the guideline says that if senior managers or directors are involved in the fraud, the auditor may see fit to go over the head of the board of directors, even non-executive directors and the audit committee, to directly report to the regulatory authorities.

Alerting the authorities would be justified if the fraud is likely to result in a material gain or loss for any one person or group of people; is likely to be 'repeated with impunity' if not disclosed; or if 'there is a general management ethic . . . of flouting the law and regulations'. The strength of the auditor's evidence is deemed important too.

Legal advice on the matter given to the APC said auditors should attach importance to the wider interests of the company in any case 'where the auditor considered that the directors could not be relied upon to apply their minds properly to those interests.'

The advice continued: 'An auditor will not be in breach of any legal duty if, although entitled to disclose, he fails to do so. His decision whether to do so or not is therefore a matter of professional judgment and not a matter of law. It is a decision which should reflect the proper expectations which the public has of his profession.'

So despite the codification of responsibilities within the guideline, it is all a matter of professional judgment. It appears that the only circumstances where the auditor of a company not in the financial sector definitely must 'blow the whistle' is when he stumbles upon treason; a practice for which there is as yet no APC guideline.

Responsibilities are different for companies covered by the special requirements of the Financial Services Act 1986, the Building Societies Act of the same year and the Banking Act 1987. Following Professor Gower's reports on Investor Protection (in 1982 and 1984), companies covered by this legislation can only be authorised to conduct business if they keep proper accounting records and have adequate internal controls.

These Acts require that auditors make specific representations to the regulators on these and other points and describe the circumstances when auditors should go directly to the authorities in order to protect the interests of shareholders or depositors.

Today's guideline – which for the first time establishes rules for auditors reporting on companies not in the financial sector – will offer solace to auditors confused about the precise nature of their duties.

The guideline makes it clear that the prime responsibility for detecting fraud rests with management. The auditor must plan an audit so that he or she has a 'reasonable expectation' of spotting serious misstatements which impinge on the truth and fairness of a set of accounts.

Thus the discovery of a major fraud after a set of accounts has been signed off is not necessary evidence that the auditors have failed to meet their responsibilities, the guideline will say. This is accurate – but hardly consolatory to companies who employ auditors or investors who rely on audited accounts which subsequently prove to be less than "true and fair".

Investors, for one, are still reeling from the implications of the verdict in the Caparo case earlier this month which, in layman's terms, said that auditors do not owe much of a duty to anybody other than existing shareholders.

Today's guideline from the APC is pitched towards the practitioner and not the business public at large. It is unlikely to do much to tackle the gulf between what the public think auditors should do and what the auditors themselves think that they are doing.

Research by KPMG Peat Marwick McLintock shows, this gap is very wide.

Peat Marwick polled 2,191 adults in the UK, of whom 122 were categorised as 'influential' (i.e. chairman, director or partner in an enterprise employing more than 50 people), and a further 232 described as 'financially aware' (owning and managing a portfolio of shares). For the accountant worried about his or her image, the results were disturbing. There was widespread ignorance of what auditors do, even on the part of people in the influential and financially aware groups.

Three-quarters of the total sample thought that it was the responsibility of auditors to check for fraud of all kinds, including 56 per cent of the influential category and 78 per cent of the financially aware group.

More than 61 per cent of the total believed that it was the responsibility of auditors to actively search for fraud, including 42 per cent of the influential and 65 per cent of the financially aware.

Other disturbing findings were that more than one third of the financially in-the-know group thought that auditors guaranteed the financial soundness of a company; and one-in-five of this group thought that audited financial statements give a very accurate or exact picture of the financial soundness of a company.

Some 27 per cent of the total thought that auditors checked between 91 and 100 per cent of all a company's financial transactions.

However, there is some good news for the much-misunderstood auditors: almost two-thirds of the top people have a favourable impression of auditors.

This compares to a mere 33 per cent who have a favourable impression of management consultants.

EXERCISE

Indicate whether the following statements are true (T) or false (F):

1. The report confirms an auditor's first responsibility of confidentiality to his client.
2. The report suggests auditors must also consider other publics.
3. Auditors should always go direct to the regulatory authorities in cases of fraud.
4. There are no cases where an auditor is legally obliged to disclose information to the authorities.
5. Most 'professional people' are aware of what auditors do.
6. An auditor's role is very often confused with that of an accountant.

3 Comprehension/interpretation

3.1 Match these three roles (the expressions are metaphors) with their best definition:

Roles	Definitions
1. Watchdog	a. Responsibility for overseeing a company's finances
2. Bloodhound	
3. Whistle-blower	b. Responsibility for informing the authorities of malpractice
	c. Responsibility for tracking down the instigators of malpractice

3.2 In what circumstances should auditors not inform management of fraud/malpractice?
3.3 Who is protected by the Financial Services Act 1986?
3.4 What do you think the Caparo case was about?
3.5 How would you summarise the responsibilities of an auditor?

4 Language focus

4.1 Mass and units (see Unit 45 in *Language Reference for Business English*)

Look at the following sentences taken from the Reading passage:

'However, there *is* some good *news* . . .'
'It is a decision which should reflect the proper expectations which the *public has* of his . . .'

Now decide whether the following words are *mass* words (they cannot be counted/can only be used in the singular) or *unit* words (they can be counted/can be used in singular and plural). Use this code: *uncountable* (U), *countable* (C).

1. equipment	8. advice
2. information	9. ethics
3. news	10. duty
4. public	11. guideline
5. fraud	12. practice
6. confidentiality	13. solace
7. ignorance	14. fairness

4.2 Obligation (see Unit 78 in *Language Reference for Business English*)

Look at the following sentence taken from the Reading passage:

'The only circumstances where the auditor . . . *must* "blow the whistle" is when he stumbles upon treason . . .'

Now use the modal verbs: **must**, **have to** and **should** to complete the sentences below:

1. It is compulsory to obey the law.
   You _____ obey the law
2. It is not a legal duty to report fraud.
   You _____ report fraud.
3. It is a moral obligation to report fraud.
   You _____ report fraud.
4. It is the prime duty of an auditor to respect a client's confidentiality.
   You _____ respect a client's confidence.
5. Auditors are advised to follow the code.
   You _____ follow the code.
6. Auditors are not allowed to be employed by a client.
   You _____ be employed by a client.

5 Word study

Match the words on the left with their best synonym on the right:

1. to alert	a. to affect
2. to stumble upon	b. consolation
3. to spot	c. to consider right
4. to give a nod and a wink	d. to state clearly
5. pro-active	e. to come across
6. to spell out	f. to warn
7. to see fit	g. to notice
8. impunity	h. to inform indirectly
9. to flout	i. initiating
10. solace	j. to openly ignore
11. to impinge upon	k. an abyss
12. a gulf	l. freedom from punishment

6 Transfer

Develop a questionnaire to clarify the role of auditors. For example:

- Do they check the accuracy of a company's accounts?
- Are they employed by the government?

When you have completed it, try it out on a number of people.

Part 2: Ethics in accounting

1 Warm-up

1.1 What are the advantages/disadvantages of valuing fixed assets at historical cost?

1.2 What should an auditor's attitude be towards deferred items which are difficult to quantify with any certainty?

2 Listening

Listen to the discussion between an auditor and a finance manager. As you listen, complete the table below.

Chart 5.3

Item	Book value/cost	Actual value/cost
Freehold property	a. _____	c. _____
Redundancy payments	b. _____	d. _____

3 Comprehension/interpretation

3.1 Why doesn't the finance manager want the assets entered into the accounts at actual value?

3.2 Why does the auditor feel they should be revalued?

3.3 What is the extraordinary item intended to cover?

3.4 Is it likely to be enough?

3.5 Why doesn't the finance manager want more set aside?

4 Language focus

4.1 Short responses (see Skill 6 in *Language Reference for Business English*)

Look at the following responses taken from the Listening passage:

'*True*, but we'd be a much bigger target . . .'
'*Good*, let me . . .'
'*Really*, then I . . .'

Now match the best responses with the statements/questions:

Statements/questions	Responses
1. Could you hand me the minutes?	a. I see
2. There are too many risks.	b. Of course not!
3. I've finished the report.	c. Maybe
4. I suppose these figures aren't accurate.	d. Never mind
5. That deals with the first part.	e. You're welcome
6. We lost the contract.	f. Good
7. Let me put it this way: it's a multiple of 50 times 3.	g. Right, let's move on
8. Could you manage a meeting at 6pm?	h. Yes, here you are
9. Thanks for all your help.	i. True

4.2 Meetings – controlling and structuring (see Skill 2 in *Language Reference for Business English*)

Look at the following extracts taken from the Listening passage:

'*There are a couple of issues I'd like to bring up.*'
'*Right, there's another issue.*'

Now match the expressions with the functions they perform:

Functions	*Expressions*
1. Outlining the structure	a. I think that covers the first point.
2. Coming to the first point	b. That's outside the scope of the meeting.
3. Closing the first point	c. Can we come to an agreement?
4. Opening the second point	d. Right, there are two major issues today . . .
5. Dealing with a digression	e. I'd like to propose . . .
6. Making a proposal	f. Before we close, let me go over the main
7. Reaching agreement	points.
8. Summarising	g. Firstly, we need to . . .
9. Closing the meeting	h. Let's call it a day.
	i. That brings us to the second major item.

5 Word study

The adjectives below can all be used to describe an auditor's work. Categorise them under the five key adjectives.

disinterested	suitable	safe	reliable	fair	logical
impartial	cautious	applicable	objective	modest	accurate
steady	unbiased	representative	appropriate	rational	true
conservative					

honest	*independent*	*relevant*	*prudent*	*consistent*
————	————	————	————	————
————	————	————	————	————
————	————	————	————	————
————	————			

6 *Transfer*

The British Institute of Chartered Accountants sets out the important concepts to be considered when working as an auditor.

First match the concepts with the appropriate explanations and then discuss which you regard as the three most important.

Concepts

1. Truth and fairness
2. Objectivity
3. Comparability
4. Relevance
5. Substance over form
6. Materiality
7. Adherence to statute
8. Evidence
9. Independence
10. Responsibility

Explanations

a. The information presented is clear to the reader
b. The accounts are prepared appropriately for the sector/industry
c. The auditors' opinions are based on facts
d. The auditor is professionally remote from his client
e. The accounts represent a true picture of the finance of the company
f. The accounts will follow conventions prescribed by law
g. The accounts, by adopting generally accepted accounting principles, can be compared with like companies
h. The accounts should reflect commercial reality not merely legal form
i. The auditor has duties to his client, third parties and under the law
j. The information should be presented without bias

UNIT 6
Taxation

Section A: Corporate and personal taxation

Part 1: Introduction to corporate taxation

1 Warm-up

1.1   What types of taxation (direct and indirect) exist in your country?
1.2   What is the effect of taxation policy on corporate investment decisions?

2 Reading

Read the following extract concerning corporate taxation. As you read it complete
Charts 6.1 and 6.2.

A well-worn saying holds that nothing is certain but death and taxes. Unhappily,
governments are often responsible for the former, and they are virtually always the
source of the latter. Since the United States is the world's largest capital market, we
will focus on taxes levied on US citizens and corporations. Most of the specific tax
rates and provisions applied in the first half of the 1980s. By far the most important
taxes for investment decision-making are personal and corporate income taxes.

CORPORATE INCOME TAX
In the US and most other countries, the corporate form of organisation is the most
important in terms of dollar value of assets owned, although many more firms are
organised as partnerships or single proprietorships. Legally, a corporation is
regarded as a separate entity, while partnerships are considered as extensions of their

Chart 6.1   Marginal and average corporate tax rates, 1983

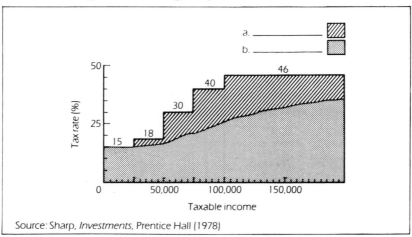

Source: Sharp, *Investments*, Prentice Hall (1978)

owners. Income earned through proprietorships and partnerships is taxed primarily through the personal tax levied on their owners. Income earned by a corporation may be taxed twice – once when it is earned via corporate income tax and again when it is received as dividends by holders of the firm's securities, via personal income tax.

CORPORATE TAX RATES

The corporate income tax is relatively simple in one respect. There are usually only a few basic rates. For example, in 1983 there was a tax rate of 15 per cent applicable on the first $25,000 of taxable income, a rate of 18 per cent applicable to the next $25,000, a rate of 30 per cent applicable to the next $25,000, 40 per cent to the next $25,000 and finally a rate of 46 per cent applicable to all income over $100,000. The result is shown in Chart 6.1 above – the top line shows the *marginal* rate, the bottom line shows the *average* tax rate. The marginal rate is more relevant for most decisions. For example, if a corporation were considering an investment that would increase its income from $65,000 to $70,000 each year, the increase in income would be $(1 - 0.3) \times \$5,000$. As the figure shows, the larger a corporation's taxable income, the closer its average tax rate comes to the higher marginal rate. Overall such corporations pay taxes equal to virtually the largest marginal rate (46 per cent).

DEFINING INCOME

For tax purposes, corporate income is defined as revenue minus expenses. The problems arise in measuring these two elements. The most dramatic instance of this difficulty concerns depreciation of assets. If a corporation buys a computer for $1 million, it is entitled to eventually charge off this cost as a deductible expense when computing taxable income. On 46 per cent rate, this represents an eventual tax saving of $460,000. The sooner the cost can be written off, the greater the benefit to the company. For the purposes of reporting corporate income to the IRS, assets are grouped into four broad classes. Automobiles and research equipment are considered *three-year property*, most business equipment is considered *five-year property*, buildings are usually considered as *fifteen-year property*.

Another vexing problem associated with the measurement of corporate income concerns the cost of inventory sold during the year. This arises when prices are changing fairly rapidly and a company holds inventory for long periods. To take a fairly simple case, imagine a retailer of sailboats. At the start of the year he has 100 in stock, all purchased for $10,000 each. During the year he takes delivery of 100 more but must pay $11,000 each, ending with 90 in stock. The boats are sold for $15,000 each. What was his income?

The question concerns the relevant cost of the 110 boats that were sold and of the 90 that remain. The firm may have sold all the 'old' boats first, or all the 'new' boats, or a mixture of the two. An accountant may assume any of the above combinations without regard to the actual facts of the situation.

Chart 6.2 The impact of different inventory valuation methods

a. Cost by _____ method	b. Cost by _____ method	c. Cost by _____ method
100 at $10,000 = $1,000,000	100 at $11,000 = $1,100,000	55 at $10,000 = $ 550,000
10 at 11,000 = 110,000	10 at 10,000 = 100,000	55 at 11,000 = 605,000
$1,110,000	$1,200,000	$1,155,000
Income $ 540,000	$ 450,000	$ 495,000
Tax (at 46%) −248,400	−207,000	−227,700
Income after tax $ 291,600	$ 243,000	$ 267,300
Cost of remaining		
inventory:		45 at $10,000
90 at $11,000 = $ 990,000	90 at $10,000 = $ 900,000	+45 at $11,000 = $ 945,000

Revenue: 110 boats at $15,000 = $1,650,000.
Source: Sharp, *Investments*, Prentice Hall (1978).

The impact of different inventory valuation methods is illustrated in Chart 6.2. When prices have been rising, the LIFO method will permit a corporation to charge more to cost in the present and less in the future. This will lower taxes in the present and raise them in the future. However, before 1970 many companies used the FIFO method, suggesting that in times of moderate inflation many managers were willing to sacrifice some real benefits to improve the appearance of their company's financial statements.

In all cases, investors should examine depreciation and inventory procedures carefully when assessing the profitability of a company.

3 Comprehension/interpretation

3.1 What are the tax advantages of a single proprietorship/partnership versus a corporation?

3.2 In what senses is corporate income liable to double taxation?

3.3 Why is the marginal rate of taxation most relevant for investment decisions?

3.4 In the US, how long does it take to depreciate a photocopier?

3.5 Why do most companies nowadays operate the LIFO inventory method?

4 Language focus

4.1 Expressing comparative relations (see Unit 50 in *Language Reference for Business English*)

Look at the following sentences taken from the Reading passage:

> '*The larger* a corporation's taxable income, *the closer* its average tax rate comes to the higher marginal rate.'
> '*The sooner* the cost can be written off, *the greater* the benefit to the company.'

Now study the four graphs in Chart 6.3 and write two sentences about each expressing a comparative relation.

Chart 6.3

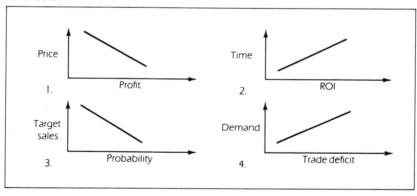

4.2 Much/many/few/little (see Unit 59 in *Language Reference for Business English*)

Look at the following sentences taken from the Reading passage:

'Although *many* more firms are organised as partnerships . . .'
'There are usually only a *few* basic rates . . .'

Now complete the sentences with one of the following:

much   many   few   little   fewer   less

1. _____ people realise how _____ tax they could avoid paying if they studied
the tax laws.
2. _____ people believe they pay too _____ tax.
3. There is too _____ time and too _____ problems to talk about irrelevant issues.
4. There isn't _____ evidence to support these figures.
5. You'll pay much _____ tax in the Cayman Islands than most places.
6. Very _____ tax authorities have clear plans for corporation tax in the future.
7. There are many _____ opportunities to avoid tax nowadays.
8. _____ companies operate the FIFO method nowadays.

5 Word study

Complete the list below:

Verb	Noun	Adjective
to govern	_____	_____
to provide	_____	_____
_____	a decision	_____
_____	_____	considerable
to apply	_____	_____
_____	depreciation	_____
to deduct	_____	_____
to assess	_____	_____
to sacrifice	_____	_____
to profit	_____	_____

6 Transfer

PAIR WORK (Partner B turn to the Key)
A: Prepare a presentation on how depreciation is calculated in your country.
     Give this explanation to your partner.

Part 2: Briefing on personal taxation

1 Warm-up

1.1   How is personal taxation structured in your country?
1.2   Is the trend in the load of personal taxation upwards or downwards?

2 Listening

Listen to the presentation about personal taxation in the UK. As you listen, complete the information in Charts 6.4 and 6.5 (referred to in the tapescript as transparencies).

Chart 6.4   Personal taxation

Rates

    Lower rate: up to £23,700:   a. _____ %

    Higher rate: above £23,700:   b. _____ %

Allowances

    Single person: c. £_____

    Married person: d. £_____

    Pensions: e. maximum _____ % of income

    Mortgage interest relief: f. _____

Chart 6.5   Collection of personal taxes

Income tax

    System: g. _____

National Insurance

    Employee's contribution: h. _____ %

    Employer's contribution: i. _____ %

3 Comprehension/interpretation

3.1   How are the two parts of Geoff's presentation structured?
3.2   What does Geoff suggest the majority think of British tax?
3.3   What new legislation has recently been introduced?
3.4   What do you think the government uses national insurance contributions for?

4 Language focus

4.1   Presentations (see Skill 1 in *Language Reference for Business English*)

Look at the following extracts from the Listening passage:

> *'Right, I'll hand you straight over to Geoff.'*
> *'Good afternoon, ladies and gentlemen . . .'*

Now match the expressions with the functions they perform in a presentation (match them under the three headings).

Functions   *Expressions*

INTRODUCTION
1. Introducing the subject   a. I've divided my presentation into two parts
2. Time limits   b. I'll try to answer your questions at the end
3. Giving an outline   c. What I'd like to do is talk to you about
4. Place of questions   d. I know you're short of time so I'll be brief

MAIN PART
1. Introducing first point   a. I'll come to that later
2. Closing first point   b. In other words
3. Referring forwards   c. As I mentioned earlier
4. Referring backwards   d. That brings me on the the next point
5. Digressing   e. So, let's start by considering
6. Moving on to next point   f. That covers my first point
7. Clarifying   g. By the way, you may be interested to know
8. Dealing with interruptions   h. If you don't mind, I'd prefer to leave that
                                                         till later

CONCLUSION
1. Summarising   a. Thank you for your attention
2. Concluding   b. I'd be delighted to answer your questions
3. Closing   c. We can draw the following conclusions
4. Inviting questions   d. So, let's just go over the main points again

5 Word study

Match the words on the left with their best synonym on the right:

1. an overview		a.	to escape
2. to get away from		b.	that is
3. to the point		c.	to choose
4. essentially		d.	boasted about
5. contrary to		e.	a summary
6. to take into account		f.	to collect
7. to opt for		g.	concise
8. i.e.		h.	fundamentally
9. vaunted		i.	by the employer
10. to levy		j.	to consider
11. at source		k.	general view
12. broad picture		l.	as opposed to

6 Transfer

Prepare and give a presentation about personal taxation in your country.

Section B: Harmonising taxation in Europe

Part 1: Tax harmonisation in Europe

1 Warm-up

1.1   What problems are created by different tax systems in different countries?

1.2   What advantages for the international company are created by different tax systems in different countries?

2 Reading

Read the following article on pan-European tax rates 'Chaos more likely than harmony' by Richard Waters. As you read it, complete Chart 6.7.

The harmonisation of taxes within the European Community is years away. The battle over indirect taxes has been heated, but is likely to fade into insignificance in the years ahead as the battleground moves to corporate taxes and, eventually, personal taxes.

Looked at in one way, this presents one of the best tax-planning opportunities that most companies will ever witness. If the internal market programme succeeds in freeing up the movement of goods, services, capital and people, then there will be considerable scope for tax 'arbitrage' – using differences in national tax systems to your advantage.

Looked at from another point of view, uncertainty over what will happen over the next ten years makes any form of business planning extremely difficult.

Alan Reid, an international tax partner at Peat Marwick McLintock, predicts fiscal chaos. 'We are moving into an area of such uncertainty that many traditional tax planning techniques are outdated. It will make tax planning, and even sensible business planning, difficult over the next ten years.'

The sort of strategic tax planning techniques now being used in European business planning are not new; they have been at the heart of international tax advice for years. But they are being given a new lease of life by the changes in business practice caused by the internal market programme.

If successful, the internal market will greatly encourage cross-border trade within the Community. This should have a major impact on corporate operations and structure; the need to be located in particular countries will diminish as it becomes easier to sell into them from outside.

Also, more companies are looking at their operations from a broader view. Rather than having functions duplicated in each country, there is a tendency to bring functions together into Community-wide operations: a single manufacturing plant, for instance, or a single marketing and distribution operation to service the entire European operation.

These structural changes create a number of tax opportunities.

The first and most obvious is the question of location. Where to put the factory or head office is a question driven mainly by factors other than tax. A skilled labour force and good communications are essential, for instance, and no amount of tax inducement can make up for a lack of these.

Language and cultural factors are equally vital.

Beyond these considerations, tax and other financial incentives come into their own. Relative tax rates, both on companies and individuals, are the most obvious influence.

All things being equal (and the internal market is an attempt to make sure that they are), companies in low-tax countries will have a competitive advantage over those in high-tax ones.

This has already begun to sink in around Europe; both West Germany and the Netherlands, in announcing plans to reduce corporate tax rates recently, have cited international competition as a prime factor in their choice.

It is hard to see where this downward pressure on tax rates will end. Countries like the UK, wishing to maintain their own tax attractions, may well push their own rates lower, sparking further rounds of tax cutting.

There is little chance of the European Commission stepping in to end this spiral. An earlier EC proposal, to bring corporation tax rates into rough alignment at 45–55 per cent, is already looking out of date. A range of 35–45 per cent may be more realistic now, though may be outmoded soon.

The competition on rates is obviously good for business, but it also creates considerable difficulty. How do you plan long or medium-term investment when there is no stability in the likely after-tax return?

Wherever possible, companies should build flexibility into their business plans to allow them to adjust to changing circumstances, says Reid.

These considerations hold true of personal as well as corporate taxes. People-intensive parts of businesses, like head offices or marketing and distribution divisions, are particularly aware of personal tax rates.

This is mainly true of companies which employ foreign nationals; most seek at least to maintain the standard of living its employees would have at home, and so meet the cost of the employees' extra tax if this is higher than at home.

US companies are a prime example. Before last year's UK budget, US employers complained that it cost them three times as much to employ a US national in London as it did in the States, largely due to the UK tax situation. With a third lopped off the top rate of income tax, they are now quiet on this subject – although proposals for changes in the way the UK taxes foreign nationals could stir up complaints again.

In addition to rates are the tax incentives designed to attract internationally mobile business. The most obvious of these are the Irish Republic's 10 per cent tax on manufacturing operations and Belgium's inducements for 'co-ordination centres', or head office operations; but there are many other incentives to encourage investment throughout the Community.

There are also other, less viable tax incentives. According to one tax adviser, it is possible to achieve the same (or even better) terms for a co-ordination centre in the UK as are available in Belgium. But because the UK's rules are a matter of negotiation rather than prescription, the incentive is not as widely noted.

Locating the various functions of a business in different countries raises a vital question: how do you split the profits of the whole operation between its constituent parts? It is in a taxpayer's interest to report most of the profit in low-tax areas. Tax authorities may well contest this.

The process of fixing prices for transactions within groups is known as transfer pricing. To taxmen these are dirty words, suggesting tax evasion: to a company they suggest important planning opportunities. They are likely to become more familiar to many more businessmen operating around Europe in the years ahead.

The opportunities for companies lie in the fact that there is never one 'correct' transfer price, but a range of possible prices all of which are commercially justifiable.

As Terry Symons, a transfer pricing specialist at Price Waterhouse, explains it, if anything between 20p and 30p is a fair commercial price for a sale between two group companies, then it is fair to pick the price best suiting the group.

Symons' advice is for directors to review transfer prices within their groups regularly (every three years) and to make sure there is adequate documentation justifying the prices picked. This could save considerable anguish in the event of any future challenge by the taxmen – and such challenges are likely to become far more frequent.

If fixing the price of tangible items is difficult, intangible ones present far greater scope for disagreement. The perception is growing – aided in the UK by the debate over 'brand accounting' – that much of a company's value lies in its intangibles, like brands or research and development. By extension, the intangible element in transfer pricing is becoming more significant. For instance, design and marketing has become a far more important element in many products. This means that more of the profit is 'made' in the territory where the design or marketing work is carried out.

Attention to this area has been speeded up by a discussion paper produced by the US Internal Revenue Service last autumn on transfer pricing and intangibles. Like all major US tax moves, this one is likely to be picked up by other authorities around the world in due course.

It is therefore worthwhile locating valuable intangibles – like brands, marketing and distribution – in low-tax areas. The location of the manufacturing operation, which can be argued to contribute relatively little to profit, becomes less significant.

According to one expert, many tax authorities around Europe have little expertise in transfer pricing. 'It's excellent news for professional tax advisers,' he says.

However, expertise is likely to develop rapidly. And in some countries there is already considerable sophistication.

Besides considerations of location and transfer pricing, the most important issue for business planners is the financial structure of their various European operations.

The fact that interest charges are tax deductible while dividends are not is a major consideration in the financial structure of an overseas subsidiary. Left to their own devices, companies would gear up in high-tax areas and keep their equity in low-tax ones. Tax authorities are aware of this practice of loading subsidiaries with debt, known as 'thin capitalisation', and have responded accordingly by denying tax relief on interest costs in some cases.

Both the US and Australia operate a policy of challenging any subsidiary with a gearing of more than three to one. Things are less clear-cut in Europe. There is a degree of concern – the UK Inland Revenue last year sought views on this subject, and its German counterpart has issued a number of discussion papers on thin capitalisation – but no hard and fast rules have yet been devised.

In the meantime, it is likely to pay companies to be cautious in the extent to which they gear up their subsidiaries.

Brian Hayes, an international tax planner at Coopers & Lybrand, reasons as follows. A financial structure of three parts debt to one part equity gives a company tax relief on 75 per cent of its financing costs. Four to one increases this proportion to 80 per cent, five to one to about 83 per cent, and so on. In other words, increasing gearing yields diminishing returns. Better to stick on gearing of three to one and avoid challenge from the tax authorities than increase it for little extra benefit.

There may be ways around the thin capitalisation problem in some countries. Take Germany, where banks receive tax relief on their investments in preference shares. This tax benefit can be passed on to the company which issues the shares, reducing its cost of finance. Since such shares count as equity, this arrangement helps to keep gearing down while securing an indirect tax advantage.

Chart 6.6 Direct corporate tax in the EC

Principal rates	Belgium	Denmark	France	W. Germany	Greece	Ireland	Italy	Luxemburg	Netherlands	Spain	UK	Portugal
Federal	43	50	39*	35/36**	40/46	47†	36	34‡	35	35 plus±	35	35
Local●	–	–	–	11/20	–	–	16	10	–	6/12	–	–

* From Jan 1 1989   † 43% from April 1 1989   ± 10% surcharge
** 36/50/46% from Jan 1 1990   ‡ From Jan 1 1989   ● Local deductible from federal
Source: CBI/Marwick Mclintock

Chart 6.7 Tax planning considerations

Location

Pricing

Financial structure

3 *Comprehension/interpretation*

3.1   What is forcing corporate tax rates downwards?
3.2   Which two countries offer clear incentives to locate?
3.3   What types of intangibles benefit from location in low-tax areas?
3.4   What are the advantages of 'thin capitalisation'?

4 *Language focus*

4.1   Noun compounds (see Unit 46 in *Language Reference for Business English*)

Look at the following sentences taken from the Reading passage:

> 'The sort of *strategic tax planning technique* now being used in *European business planning* . . .'
> 'In addition to rates are the tax incentives designed to attract *internationally mobile business*.'

Now make effective noun compounds from the following phrases:

1. Documentation which has been prepared well and is informative.
2. A consultant from Germany working in the field of taxation with good qualifications.
3. A company, based in Switzerland which manufactures watches and makes high profits.
4. Competition which is unfair and has been growing rapidly.
5. Tax rates applying in Europe which are aligned unequally.

4.2   Similarity and difference (see Unit 72 in *Language Reference for Business English*)

Look at the following sentences taken from the Reading passage:

'*All things being equal*, . . . companies in low-tax countries will have a tax advantage over those in high-tax ones.'
'*Like* all major US tax moves, this one is likely to be picked up . . .'

Now complete the following text by using the words/expressions below:

like	as	unlike	different	differ
the same	similar	variety	vary	in common

1. _____ many major European cities, London is an expensive place to live.
2. Inventory levels were _____ forecast.
3. Although they have much _____, they _____ in vital ways; for example the two companies have a totally _____ structure.
4. There is a tremendous _____ of tax incentives. However, in one sense, they are _____ to each other in that they are all difficult to understand.
5. In the UK we all pay _____ rate of corporation tax; _____ in Germany where rates _____ from 35 to 56 per cent.

5 Word study

Match the expressions on the left with their closest equivalent on the right:

1. to fade into insignificance
2. to give a new lease of life
3. to sink in
4. to spark
5. outmoded
6. to stir up
7. to be left to your own devices
8. hard and fast rules
9. at the heart of
10. to make up for
11. all things being equal
12. dirty words

a. in the centre
b. out-of-date
c. strict regulations
d. to be realised
e. to compensate for
f. to diminish
g. to be free to act
h. if all variables can be ignored
i. to revive
j. unacceptable expressions
k. to initiate
l. to create

6 Transfer

Use the information in the Reading passage (including the tax rate table, Chart 6.6) to discuss the following case.

Name of company:	Whole Health Company (WHC)
Industry:	Health-care products
Head office:	London
Manufacturing:	UK, Ireland, Germany
Sales subsidiaries:	All European countries
Branded products:	Developed and marketed from the UK

In the post-1992 European market, WHC needs to make decisions about manufacturing, sales and head office locations. What are the tax considerations they should be aware of?

Part 2: Plant location decisions

1 Warm-up

1.1 What are the prime factors which must be taken into account when deciding on the location of a new factory?

1.2 How would you rank these factors in order of importance?

2 Listening

Listen to an extract from a meeting in which the location of a new plant is the issue under discussion. As you listen, complete Chart 6.8 which is referred to during the meeting as a transparency.

Chart 6.8

	Communication	Labour force	Plant construction	Manufacturing cost	Tax benefits
Scotland France Germany					

1 = best score   2 = medium score   3 = worst score

3 Comprehension/interpretation

3.1 What is meant by communications?
3.2 What are the two aspects of labour force to be considered?
3.3 Why should a manufacturing plant be regarded as a cost rather than a profit centre?
3.4 How could prices be structured internally to take advantage of varying tax rates?

4 Language focus

4.1 Questions – softening (see Unit 38 in *Language Reference for Business English*)

Look at the following questions from the Listening passage:

'Just before you move onto tax, *can I ask you about* the plant construction?
'*I was wondering whether* any of the countries we are considering . . .'

Make the following direct questions more indirect/softer:

1. What about tax incentives?
2. Do they offer help with investment?
3. Did the tax authorities advise you about transfer prices?
4. How much does the land cost?
5. Have you included the tax weighting in your calculations?
6. What do the rest of you think?
7. Are you thinking of siting the plant in Scotland?
8. Why won't you consider Germany?

4.2 Clarifying (see Unit 73 in *Language Reference for Business English*)

Look at the following extracts taken from the Listening passage:

'The third factor is the plant construction cost, *i.e.* the initial investment cost.'
'*What do you mean? – Well, simply* . . .'

Now complete the dialogue below:

A: We've been trying hard to avoid double taxation?
B: _____ mean?
A: _____ paying tax twice – first in the country of payment and secondly in the country of residence.
B: So, if _____ correctly, you _____ the expatriate workers could have to pay tax here in Saudi and again back in the US.
A: That's _____. We have approached the US tax authorities and it seems there is a double taxation agreement between the two countries but it is time dependent . . .
B: _____ slowly?
A: Of course, what I _____ was that it is possible to avoid double taxation but it depends on how long the expatriate works in Saudi. Now, most of our contracted workers are on short contract varying from 60 to 120 days. The US tax authorities are prepared to waive tax after six months.
B: So are you _____ that our guys are going to have pay tax twice.
A: Yes, but it could be redeemable _____ they could get the tax back later . . .

5 *Word study*

Study the expressions used to *rank* locations:

first	scores highest	way/slightly ahead	on top
second	in the middle	way/just behind	
third	scores lowest	lagging behind	at the bottom

plus: there's little to choose between
to come down in favour of

Using the following information, complete the sentences below.

	Literacy	Numeracy	Personality	Experience
Jane	++	+	+++	–
Susan	+	++	+	+
Tessa	+++	–	++	+

1. Jane _____ highest in terms of _____.
2. She _____ the others in experience.
3. Susan is _____ Jane in terms of literacy but _____ on numeracy.
4. There's _____ Susan and Tessa in terms of experience.
5. Tessa comes out _____ in literacy.

6 *Transfer*

Look back at Chart 6.8. Go over the factors again in discussion. Try to reach a decision based on the information you have available.

UNIT 7
Valuation

Section A: New approaches to valuation

Part 1: The value of brands

1 Warm-up

1.1   Are a company's historical results a good indicator of future performance?
1.2   How can a company value the potential of new products in their accounts?

2 Reading

Read the following article 'Wrong figures lead to wrong decisions' by David Waller. As you read it, complete Chart 7.1.

Mention brand accounting to a finance director or stockbroker's analyst, and the likelihood is that there will follow a disquisition on the ingenious way that companies like Grand Metropolitan, Guinness and Rank Hovis McDougall have managed to bolster their balance sheets by ascribing a value to their brand portfolios.

There is, however, another, less familiar side to the brand accounting debate: namely, over the way in which companies measure the performance of their brands internally and decide how to allocate resources from one brand to another. According to a recent report from David Allen, a former finance director of Cadbury, the confectionery manufacturer, and now a professor at Loughborough University, the misuse of accounting is leading to the mismanagement of brands.

Allen's thesis – to be found in the report *Creating Value: The Financial Management of Brands* – is simple but damning. Having talked to numerous British managers in companies with brand portfolios, he argues that traditional double-entry accounting is being used 'beyond its "design spec"' to assess whether a brand is doing well or badly, and that as a result managers are taking the wrong investment decisions.

He draws a contrast between two different ways of measuring financial performance. The first is the accounting model which forms the basis of the figures one finds in a company's formal report and accounts. This, Allen argues, is designed for 'stewardship reporting', ie giving a picture of the company's financial performance to its shareholders. Inevitably, argues Allen, such figures are backward-looking, focusing on tangible assets and realised profits.

In contrast to this, there is what Allen calls 'pro-active financial management'. This, he explains, involves 'forward-looking subjective judgments', often based on intangible values, i.e. on gains which are as yet unrealised and thus do not find their way into a set of financial accounts.

The central problem, according to Allen's scheme of things, is that the management accounts used by those directly responsible for a portfolio of brands are no more than 'sub-sets of financial accounts'. The management accounts 'are more frequent,' he explains, 'and more detailed, but are primarily used to check that the business is on course for its target profits. The danger that [the brand's] long-term health may thereby be damaged is hardly ever quantified.'

This stems from short-termism at the very top of the company, Allen argues: 'Directors of public companies say they believe that their security depends on reported results. Middle and junior management are motivated to support them by means of objectives, performance measures and rewards, expressed in terms of accounting profits (or derivatives, such as return on assets or earnings per share).'

Thus, Allen continues: 'Investments in brand-building strategies are explained, not in terms of what can be justified on the basis of expected returns, but in terms of what can be afforded on the basis of reported profits.'

Expenditure – on research, development, training, marketing and information management – may thus be seen as no more than an appropriation of forecast profits, rather than as the vital investment required to maintain the strength of the brand over the long term. Moreover, Allen finds, marketing expenditure is often seen as the most discretionary outlay under management control.

'Problems in other parts of the mix (volume, price, cost) are compensated for by reducing marketing support, so as to stay on course for the profit figure which is seen as a commitment – and is used as the benchmark for bonus calculations . . . Quite frequently, support for one brand is reduced in order to compensate for volume, price or cost problems faced by another . . .'

What is required, according to Allen, is a new accounting model which recognises the importance of intangible assets and unrealised gains – a model which represents the net present value of the cash which will flow from that brand over the medium-term, a statement of the total wealth of the business independent of the exigencies of the stock market and financial reporting.

In the penultimate chapter of his report, Allen advocates the use of a system based on an estimate of the present value of the business. This would enable managers to overcome traditional accounting's distinction between capital expenditure (which bolsters the balance sheet) and revenue expenditure (which is set off against profits).

'Fundamentally,' Allen says, 'there is no difference between the two outlays; the cash used to defray what the accountant calls capital expenditure is the same as that used to defray revenue expenditure. Buying market share [by spending on advertising, which would reduce reported profits] is no different from buying the plant with which to supply it.'

It is not as simple as this, though; the present value calculations must be adjusted to take account of (a) 'interactions' and (b) 'relativity'. In this context, interaction means the way the demand stimulated by the advertising is exploited, i.e. as higher volume or higher price. Relativity refers to 'the relative advertising effectiveness which builds relative market standing, and relative price which translates this into market share and volume.'

What do finance directors think of Allen's ideas? A good one to turn to is Neville Bain, finance director of Cadbury-Schweppes, parent company of Cadbury itself. Bain says he sympathises with Allen's analysis, but is not convinced that his former colleague offers a practicable solution to the problems of accounting and short-termism.

'Cash is a reality, profit a matter of opinion,' says Bain. 'Even so, we hardly ever use discounted cash flow analysis to measure performance at the trading level, although we may use it to assess whether we should buy a company or start the same business from scratch. I have to agree with David that the bonuses for the managing directors of our average businesses are calculated largely by reference to short-term trading profits.

'Whether our brands suffer as a result of the cutting of marketing expenditure is a different matter,' Bain continues. 'It's almost too obvious a trick to get profits up by cutting advertising expenditure.'

He thinks it important that good business performance be reflected in terms that the providers of the company's capital can understand. Nevertheless, he is sympathetic to the argument that the performance-measurement model should, somehow, take account of subjective, non-financial criteria.

Quite how is another matter; Bain says that Allen's model is too complicated for ready implementation.

Chart 7.1

Traditional approach	New approach
Stewardship reporting	(i) _____
Backward-looking	(ii) _____
Measurement using: Management accounts	Measurement using: (iii) _____
Short-termism	(iv) _____

Reductions in marketing
    expenditure
	Assessment of:
	    Interactions
	(v) _____

Reported profits used
    as a benchmark for
    bonus calculations
	Potential profits
	    used as a benchmark?

3 Comprehension/interpretation

3.1 What is the normal perception of brand accounting?
3.2 Why, in the view of Mr Allen, is traditional accounting not suitable for the internal financial management of brands?
3.3 What is meant by short-termism?
3.4 Why do you think marketing expenditure is the most discretionary outlay?
3.5 In what sense are capital and revenue expenditure the same?
3.6 How do you think interactions and relativity can be calculated?
3.7 What are Mr Bain's conclusions about the new model?

4 Language focus

4.1 Modals – overview (see Units 17–19 in *Language Reference in Business English*)

Look at the following sentences taken from the Reading passage:

'The danger that long-term health *may* be damaged . . .'
'The present value calculations *must* be adjusted to take account of . . .'
'I *have to* agree with David that the bonuses . . .'

Now choose from the modal verbs below in order to complete the dialogue:

must   may   can   have to   could   should

A: Surely your brands _____ be worth more than that?
B: Well, it's very difficult to say. They _____ well be. However, we prefer to put it on the conservative side.

A: I _____ say I find these figures hard to believe. After all, a company that wanted to create a brand would _____ pay a fortune in advertising alone.

B: Yes, that's true, but you _____ not put a figure on brand creation – it depends on so many factors.

A: I agree, but we _____ calculate from a historical basis.

B: That's not the point. The real value is the long-term potential profits. How _____ you estimate them?

A: Well, you _____ have annual sales forecasts?

B: Of course, but if we're going to value them in the balance sheet, we _____ have a longer-term perspective.

A: In my opinion what you _____ do is take ten years' potential net income and . . .

4.2   Reporting verbs (see Unit 25 in *Language Reference for Business English*)

Look at some of the phrases taken from the Reading passage:

> '*He says . . .*'
> '*He explains . . .*'
> '*He continues . . .*'
> '*He advocates . . .*'
> '*He is not convinced . . .*'

Now match the following reporting verbs to the statements below:

S/he   a. argued
        b. thought
        c. concluded
        d. explained
        e. announced
        f. contradicted
        g. summarised
        h. agreed
        i. disagreed
        j. wondered

1. I really can't agree with you.
2. All staff can take a holiday tomorrow.
3. The net profit figure is calculated by deducting overheads from the gross profit.
4. You say it'll take two weeks. I reckon twice as long.
5. The only conclusion you can reach is that we have to get out of the market.
6. I'm with you 100 per cent.
7. To recap then, there are two main points we have discussed.
8. I sometimes ask myself why I took on this project.
9. In my opinion, we should leave immediately.
10. There are two sides: on the one hand, we should consider our costs; on the other, we have good prospects of long-term profits.

5 Word study

Complete the sentences below by inserting one of the following words in the spaces provided:

practicable   defray   bolster   stems
discretionary   allocate   ascribe   appropriate
ingenious   tricks

1. They used the revaluation of the land to ____ their balance sheet.
2. He was worried that the bonus should be paid to everybody. I assured him that it was ____.
3. He has developed an ____ way of reducing his tax bill.
4. It's difficult to ____ value to a brand.
5. We must ____ more resources to his new development.
6. I think the problem ____ from poor management.
7. I'm afraid there are no easy ____. It's just a question of hard work.
8. We have to ____ profits from this sector to support the other.
9. Your solution is interesting but not ____.
10. The fund was used to ____ unexpected expenses.

6 Transfer

- Do you think a new accounting model is necessary for the financial management of brand portfolios?
- In what ways can a company motivate its managers in the medium rather than short term?

Part 2: Forecasting future performance

1 Warm-up

1.1 What are the periods of greatest investment during a product's life cycle?
1.2 Can investment in marketing halt the usual decline towards the end of a product's life?

2 Listening

Listen to a product manager presenting forecasts for the two products he is responsible for. As you listen, complete Charts 7.2 and 7.3.

Chart 7.2   Projected turnover

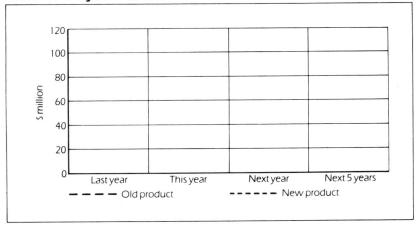

Chart 7.3   Projected profits

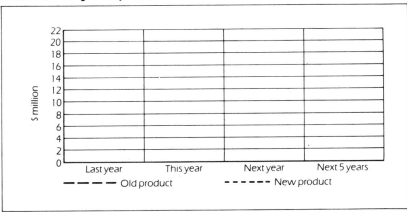

3   Comprehension/interpretation

3.1   What is the objective of this presentation?

3.2   What is Phison's decline due to?

3.3   Why does he forecast a decline in Superphison's turnover so early in its life?

3.4   How will they manage to steady profits of Phison next year?

3.5   Why will there be a plateau in Superphison's profits next year?

3.6   What is his conclusion?

4 Language focus

4.1 Describing trends (see Unit 68 in *Language Reference for Business English*)

Look at the following extracts from the Listening passage:

'This year we have started to see a *steady* decline . . .'
'Next year this downward trend is likely to continue, but not so *steeply*.'

Now match the adjectives (a–l) with the categories below (one has been done for you in each case):

1. Angle of decline: *steep*
2. Size of decline: *great*
3. Speed of decline: *slow*
4. Regularity of decline: *steady*
5. Significance of decline: *marked*

a. dramatic	d. considerable	g. moderate	j. significant
b. rapid	e. gentle	h. sharp	k. noticeable
c. erratic	f. gradual	i. slight	l. constant

4.2 Describing graphs (see Unit 68 in *Language Reference for Business English*)

Look at the following extracts from the Listening passage:

'The *broken line* represents Phison, *the dotted* Superphison.'
'. . . on *the horizontal axis* we have the same time periods, whilst on *the vertical axis* . . .'

Now match the terms below with their reference points on Chart 7.4.

Chart 7.4

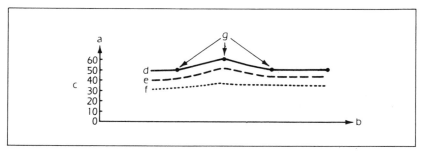

1. scale
2. solid line
3. vertical axis
4. broken line
5. plots (plotted)
6. horizontal axis
7. dotted line

5 Word study

Match the words/expressions with the correct figure:

a. stable   f. constant   k. upward trend
b. steep   g. gradual   l. level
c. plateau   h. rapid   m. sharp
d. peak   i. gentle   n. steady
e. downward trend   j. stagnant   o. dramatic

Chart 7.5

Chart 7.6

Chart 7.7

Chart 7.8

Chart 7.9

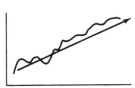

Chart 7.10

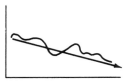

6 *Transfer*

PAIR WORK (Partner B turn to the key)
A: (i) Describe Chart 7.11a to your partner so that s/he can plot it accurately.
    (ii) Now listen to your partner's presentation of a graph. Use the information to recreate his/her graph in Chart 7.11b.

Chart 7.11a Project profitability

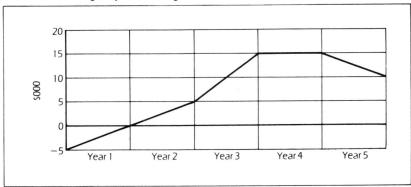

Chart 7.11b

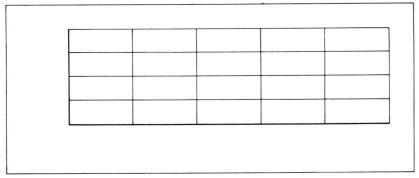

Section B: Company ratings and failure

Part 1: Valuation and business failure

1 *Warm-up*

1.1 What are the early warning signs that a business is going to fail?
1.2 How can an investor protect him/herself from the risk of business collapse?

2 Reading

Read the article about two recent business failures. As you read it, complete the information in Chart 7.12.

This is the story of two 'successful' companies. One publishes a glossy set of accounts in June 1990 showing record profits, strong dividend growth and a healthy balance sheet. Ten months later, before it can produce another annual report, it goes bust. The second company produces an even more spectacular set of accounts in July 1990, followed six months later by a near doubling of interim earnings and a two-thirds rise in dividend. It too goes bust.

Both companies – Parkroll and Colfield – are victims not of external disaster but of their own uncontrolled growth. So what is there in their published financial history to warn of coming disaster. Remarkably little, on the face of it. Both companies had a big enough market value at their peak – Colfield £280m, Parkroll £430m. But, even now, with hindsight, it's hard to detect the seeds of collapse. In Colfield's last accounts, balance sheet gearing jumped from 8 per cent to 35 per cent. But interest cover stayed remarkably high at 8.5 times. Parkroll's gearing went from 20 per cent to 65 per cent: but again interest cover was seemingly safe at 4.5 times.

The traditional financial ratios showed grounds for slight caution, but no more than might be expected in the early days of an economic downturn. Parkroll's liquidity ratio (liquid assets to current liabilities) dropped last year from 1.5 times to 1.4; but it had earlier been much lower. The same ratio dipped alarmingly in Colfield's case from 1.5 to 1.1; but in textbook terms, even a liquidity ratio of 1 is normally regarded as healthy.

Other measurements indicated the same modest deterioration; the stock/turnover ratio, for instance, or the ratio of trade debtors to creditors. But both companies showed positive net operational cash flow in their last flow of funds statements. And both made the traditional statement of managerial confidence by increasing the dividend; Colfield by 15 per cent and Parkroll by 70 per cent.

It has to be said that Colfield in particular had a long-standing reputation for creative accounting. In its last accounts, for instance, it took a sharp-eyed reader of the notes to spot that in selling off a couple of subsidiaries to management buyouts in order to reduce its debts, Colfield had largely financed the buyouts itself. One of them then went bust and so did Colfield. In keeping with this reputation is the fact that Colfield's share price started to fall a good two years before its published profits did. In Parkroll's case, the process was more rapid but similar in principle. From their January peak of 520p, Parkroll's shares lost 470p before last week's suspension. But, of that fall, more than a third took place before the July profit warning which was the first formal notice that something was wrong.

It is here that the chief moral lies. It is plain that in such cases the audited accounts give shareholders no inkling of what is really happening. The market's response is pragmatic. The share price has been at odds with figures and the share price has been proved right. The natural conclusion is that it is the only reliable guide around. The snag is that this can be a vicious circle. If the share price is trying to tell you something, the logical response is to sell the shares. The price then drops further, which means it is telling you something more, and so on.

If the company is not in fact going bust, the result is overshoot. This seems to be the case with Amford, which plunged horribly for eighteen months before touching bottom last December. Since then it has out-performed the market by nearly 60 per cent. The same may yet prove to be the case with the most mysterious collapsing share of them all, Canford Electronics, which has under-performed the market by nearly 70 per cent in the past eighteen months and is still falling. It remains the case that for public companies suddenly to collapse under a burden of unsuspected debt is a very worrying development. It has become commonplace to observe that the asset side of the average balance sheet has been so distorted by years of inflation and goodwill write-offs as to be almost meaningless. The liabilities side ought to be another matter; but, just when it is most needed, it seems to have become meaningless as well.

Chart 7.12

	Colfield	Parkroll
Peak market value		
Balance sheet gearing		
Interest cover		
Liquidity ratios		
Net operational cash flow		
Dividends		

3 Comprehension/interpretation

3.1   What is the importance of interest cover when assessing a company's gearing?
3.2   What do you think is a healthy liquidity ratio?
3.3   What is meant by creative accounting?
3.4   Why is there a snag in using share price as an indicator of company strength?
3.5   How do you think a balance sheet should be adjusted to be more meaningful?

4 Language focus

4.1 Past time – past perfect (see Unit 7 in *Language Reference for Business English*)

Look at the following sentences taken from the Reading passage:

> 'Parkroll's liquidity ratio . . . dropped last year from 1.5 times to 1.4; but it *had* earlier *been* much lower.'
> 'In selling off a couple of subsidiaries . . ., Colfield *had* largely *financed* the buyouts itself.'

Now complete the following sentences by putting the verbs either in the past simple or past perfect.

1. We _____ not (want) to see the accounts because we _____ already (see) them.
2. When the figures _____ (arrive), they _____ already (draft) twice.
3. The office _____ (be) very quiet when I _____ (visit) it. Everybody _____ (go) home.
4. The company _____ (publish) some excellent results last year. Later, it _____ (go) bust.
5. The company _____ (report) an upturn in profits last month. Earlier in the year, it _____ (announced) declining sales.
6. There _____ (be) two major company collapses last week. Both companies _____ (try) to avoid bankruptcy.

4.2 **Too/both/either** (see Unit 60 in *Language Reference for Business English*)

Look at the following sentences taken from the Reading passage:

> 'It *too* goes bust.'
> '*Both* companies are victims not of external disaster . . .'

Complete the following sentences with **too, both, either, neither**:

1. I think this company is going to go bust. – I do _____.
2. He didn't think the results were good. I didn't _____.
3. _____ of us had invested in Parkroll. We _____ lost a lot of money.
4. _____ companies grew rapidly. _____ controlled their growth.
5. Which company are you going to invest in? _____, I don't really mind.
6. Which company are you going to invest in? _____, they are _____ in unstable markets.

5 Word study

Reread the Reading passage. Find those words/expressions that can be categorised as connected with either success or failure. Group them under these two headings. Some examples have already been entered.

Success	*Failure*
record profits	to go bust
strong growth	disaster
_____	_____
_____	_____
_____	_____
_____	_____
_____	_____
_____	_____
	_____
	_____

6 Transfer

- Should the regulatory authorities insist that balance sheets are more representative of a company's financial position?
- In the cases above, what other indicators would you have liked to have seen if you had been an investor?

Part 2: Discussion of privatisation

1 Warm-up

1.1 Do you think privatisation of nationalised infrastructure industries (e.g. telecommunications, post, railways) makes good financial and commercial sense?

1.2 What is the policy towards privatisation pursued by your country's government?

2 Listening

Listen to the extract from a TV panel discussion about privatisation. As you listen, complete Chart 7.13.

Chart 7.13

	Arguments in favour	Arguments against
Political		
Financial		
Industrial		
Social		

3 Comprehension/interpretation

3.1 How can it be argued that privatisation ties the shareholder to the Tory party?

3.2 Many privatisations are preceded by write-offs of long-term government debts. Do you think this gives the newly privatised companies an unfair competitive advantage?

3.3 Why are civil servants more likely than business people to protect the long-term interest of the nation?

3.4 Peter Smythe admits that British Telecom privatisation was beneficial for some. Whom?

3.5 What type of elector is Peter Smythe representing?

3.6 What does Peter Smythe's sarcastic remark about BT's public relations suggest?

4 Language focus

4.1 Presentations – introducing subjects (see Skill 1 in *Language Reference for Business English*)

Look at the following extracts taken from the Listening passage:

'We're here tonight to discuss the pros and cons . . .'
'On the political side, we have . . .'
'On the financial front, . . .'
'From an industrial point of view . . .'

Now match the subject introduction with the content notes:

Subject introduction	Content
1. As far as the economy is concerned	a. the ecosystem, pollution, ozone
2. From a social point of view	b. the government in power, opposition
3. Looking at it from a political standpoint	c. profit and loss, depreciation
4. On the financial front	d. trade deficit, GNP
5. On the subject of the environment	e. employment, housing education

4.2 Relative clauses (see Unit 39 in *Language Reference for Business English*)

Look at the following extract taken from the Listening passage:

'There are those *who* believe that water, telecommunications and gas, to name but three, have all been successful privatisation issues *which* have led to major restructuring and financing . . .'

Now combine the following sentences:

1. There are twenty people. They are waiting outside. They have been invited to the show.
2. The government spokesman. He comes from the Finance Ministry. He is going to speak on the programme.
3. Telecommunications was privatised six years ago. It has always been very profitable.
4. The government has followed a policy of privatisation. It was first elected eleven years ago.
5. Peter Smythe is an opposition spokesman on Trade and Industry. Peter Smythe starts the discussion.

5 Word study

Complete the expressions by matching left and right columns:

1. asset	a. prices
2. to set	b. in the hands of
3. popular	c. for improvement
4. selling off	d. but three
5. rock-bottom	e. with the details
6. vested	f. by advertisements
7. to name	g. stripping
8. suffer	h. the nation's silver
9. to leave	i. success
10. rip-roaring	j. forward
11. bore you	k. the rigours
12. great strides	l. great store by
13. room	m. capitalism
14. taken in	n. interest

6 Transfer

Use Chart 7.13 to discuss the pros and cons of privatisation.

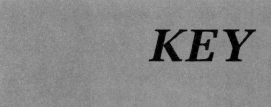

KEY

UNIT 1
The financial climate

Part 1: World economic climate

2 *Reading*

Chart 1.

Interest rates	↗
Output	↘
Inflation	↗
US c/a deficit	↗
Japan c/a surplus	↗
German c/a surplus	↗

3 *Comprehension/interpretation*

3.1 An economy that moves cyclically from boom to recession without stability.

3.2 The crisis is caused by the fact that many third world and developing countries are unable to repay loans from the developed world.

3.3 Because Americans will buy a lot of imported goods.

3.4 Import quotas, tariffs, etc.

3.5 A relatively painless move from high growth to recession where factors like unemployment are not too badly affected.

4 *Language focus*

4.1 Tense review

1. Inflation has increased steadily this year.
2. Unemployment peaked last year and since then has gone down.
3. As the international debt crisis grows, the world economy becomes more unstable.
4. The IMF carried out a study last year. In this study they projected a decline in GNP in most countries.
5. The world economy seems to be going into a decline.
6. If Japan's current account surplus increases further it will cause even more instability in the world economy.
7. The state of international trade remains a worry. Projections for the rest of the nineties bring very little hope.
8. We are studying the effect of the fall in the dollar's value at the moment.
9. We would have preferred more stability if that had been possible.
10. For more than ten years the value of the US dollar has fallen/has been falling. Before that, it was/had been one of the stronger currencies.

5 Word study

5.1

growth	U	decline	D
recovery	U	fall	D
jump	U	rise	U
drop	D	increase	U

5.2

1. grew
2. fell . . . recovered . . . rose
3. declined . . . increase
4. fallen

NOTE: Other answers are possible.

Part 2: Key indicators

Listening tapescript

I'd like to look at two indicators and how they have affected our sales this year.

If you look at this first graph, I've plotted domestic and export sales. As you can see, domestic sales, represented by the solid line here, have remained pretty constant for most of the year – around £40 million a month. There were two slight dips – one in April to £36 million, and the other in August to £37 million – but I'll come back to these later.

Now, export sales, shown here by the broken line, have fluctuated quite wildly during the year. They started the year around £65 million and rose in the first quarter to a new record of £82 million. They levelled off for a month or so and then started to fall dramatically to reach a low of £45 million in June. They recovered a bit over the next few months and seemed to find their level around £55 million for the last three months of the year.

Now some, not all of course, of these changes can be explained by contrasting our export sales figures with the value of the dollar. This is shown here on the second graph by the broken line. As you know, all exports are invoiced in dollars. Now, at the end of last year the dollar stood at around 1.5. During January, the dollar fell to a new low of 1.45 and then stuck at around this level for the next three months of the year. The lower value certainly helped to make us very competitive on the European market. In March the dollar started to rise again and reached 1.75 in May. Since then it has been pretty stable around this level. So, in conclusion, we are very vulnerable to changes in the dollar value. As one would expect, there's a delay factor of two to three months as the price changes trickle through to our customers, but basically when the dollar comes down, we are very competitive; when it's up we are clearly struggling.

Finally, this other solid line shows consumer prices – a measure of inflation over the year – as you can see, there's a slight upward trend and, noticeably, two sudden jumps – one in March, the other in July when interest rates were raised by 1 per cent each time. This clearly had an impact on our domestic sales – if you remember the slight dips in April and August – here on the previous graph . . .

Chart 1.3

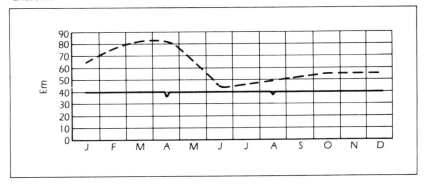

Chart 1.4

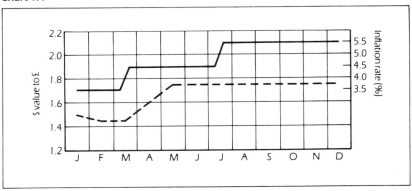

3 Comprehension/interpretation

3.1 Because it is an international currency, traded throughout the world.

3.2 The value of the dollar could be affected by interest rate changes, political uncertainty, state of the American/British economies.

3.3 It will always take time for price changes to become effective for the customer.

3.4 Because the cost of money would be higher, leaving customers with less disposable income.

4 Language focus

4.1 Present perfect and past simple

1. At the end of last year the dollar stood at 1.5.
2. Last January the dollar fell to a new low of 1.45.
3. Since then it has been pretty stable.
4. As you can see on this graph, I've plotted domestic and export sales.
5. Export sales have fluctuated pretty wildly.
6. We haven't yet seen the full effect of the declining dollar.
7. Last quarter we saw one of the best results.

8. We've already noticed a slight drop in orders.
9. The low profit margins were reflected in last year's figures.
10. We've received two big orders so far this quarter.

4.2 Past reference

1. Over/During/In the last few months, sales have been disappointing.
2. We have been expecting an upturn since the beginning of the year.
3. At the end of last year, there was a sudden downturn.
4. He was appointed finance director two years ago and since then he has reduced the staff by 200.
5. We went through a difficult period in/during the middle of April.
6. The computer system crashed in/during/over the holidays.
7. We have raised prices in line with inflation for three years.
8. The dips in the price index happened in April and July.

5 Word study

1.h   2.i   3.j   4.a   5.d   6.e   7.b   8.g   9.f   10.c

6 Transfer

B: (i)   Listen to your partner's presentation and plot the information on Chart 1.6c.
          (ii)   Describe the information shown in Chart 1.6d so that your partner can plot it on his/her graph.

Chart 1.6c

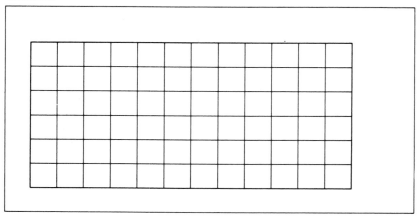

Chart 1.6d Exchange rate fluctuations

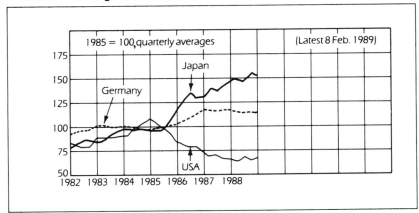

UNIT 2
Funding the business

Section A: Sources of funds

Part 1: Gearing

2 *Reading*

Chart 2.1

	Source of funds	Advantages/disadvantages
Low gearing	(i) Owner's capital	Most exposed but claim on all profits
	(ii) Venture capital	Demand very high rate of return but doesn't interfere in company
	(iii) Unlisted security market	Outside investors, no loss of control
	(iv) Stock exchange	Long-term solution to raising money 25% in public hands therefore less control
High gearing	Long-term loans from banks and pension funds	Secured over fixed assets Better return on net profits in prosperous times High interest payments in difficult times

3 *Comprehension/interpretation*

Up to you!

4 *Language focus*

4.1 Comparison of adjectives

1. It's much harder to raise money on the Stock Exchange.
2. Increasing owner's capital is the riskiest way of raising money for investment.
3. The banks will be more cautious than the securities markets.
4. Interest rates are much higher this year than last.
5. The safest method of increasing working capital is to plough back profits.
6. A fixed-term loan is less flexible than a fluctuating overdraft.
7. On the other hand, a medium-term loan is easier to control than a fluctuating overdraft.
8. Venture capital is much more difficult to raise than we are led to believe.
9. The Stock exchange rules are much more formal than the USM.
10. Expansion is more attractive in times of low interest rates.

4.2 Contrast

1. Sutton Savings Bank offers a small and friendly service. On the other hand, it has no solid experience.

---

2. First National Bank has a solid track record. However, it is very impersonal.
3. Trust Financial Services offers an attractive venture capital scheme. On the other hand, loans are fixed at high interest rates.
4. Welcome Investments Ltd offers low interest rates but is limited to low maximum capital sums.

NOTE: These are only model answers. Other versions are possible.

5 *Word study*

Verbs	*Nouns (concept)*	*Nouns (agent)*
to survive	survival	a survivor
to prosper	prosperity	
to bankrupt	bankruptcy	
to provide	provision	a provider
to interfere	interference	
to invest	investment	an investor
to secure	security	
to earn	earnings	
to own	ownership	an owner

Part 2: Negotiating a loan

Listening tapescript

A: We've been short of space for some time now and finally we've decided we must move to bigger premises. We've looked at a number of properties in the area and come down in favour of this one in the centre of town.

B: How much are they asking for it?

A: £300,000. But we think we'll get it for £280,000.

B: I see. That's a major investment for a firm of your size.

A: We realise that, but we see it as a valuable resource for the business which will help us to expand, and at the same time a sound investment.

B: I understand. Are you looking for a loan to cover the total price?

A: Well, we've considered that. We could raise £50,000 by cutting back on management bonuses and one or two investment projects.

B: But ideally you'd like to borrow the full £300,000?

A: That's right.

B: What sort of term were you thinking of?

A: Well, either fifteen or twenty years. Could you give me a quote for both terms?

B: Yes, just a moment . . . I'll check my tables. Well, over fifteen years on fully fluctuating interest it'd be £3,500 a month, that's based on 2 per cent above current base rate. And over twenty years it'd be £3,000 a month.

A: Yes, that's roughly what we calculated. I think we'd prefer the twenty year loan.

B: Right, let's come back to that. Have you brought some up-to-date figures for me?

A: Yes, I have. As you can see, turnover is up on last year by about 20 per cent and profits look like being even better – about 25 per cent higher than last year. That means a net profit of around £30,000.

B: That sounds very healthy. Have you done any projections?

A: Yes, we have. As you know, it's difficult to forecast accurately in our line of business, but we reckon turnover should continue to increase at this sort of rate for the next five years and our margins, if anything, should get better.

B: Good, perhaps you can leave the figures with me?

A: Of course.

B: What worries me is your cash flow – at present you're operating at close to the limit of your £50,000 facility – in fact, sometimes you're straying the wrong side of it. Do you see any improvement in that area?

A: Well, as you know, in our line of business, we're always going to have a cash flow problem. As we expand, it's difficult to avoid pushing up the need for working capital.

B: I realise that but you're thinking of taking on an additional major drain on cash. On the present figures, you may well have problems financing the payments.

A: We're confident we can get the sales to justify this investment. Also I'm sure you'll find the security on the building is more than enough. We've had the property valued and been told it's worth at least £350,000. On top of that, our fixed assets stand at £75,000 on the last balance sheet.

B: That's true but what worries me is your current liabilities – to the bank and also your current creditors. According to these figures, that stands at nearly £90,000.

2 Listening

Reason for loan:	property (short of space)
Amount of loan:	£300,000
Term of loan:	20 years
Interest rate:	2 per cent above current base rate
Current instalment:	£3,000 per month
Security: type:	property
market value:	£350,000
Turnover:	up 20 per cent
Profits:	up 25 per cent (30,000)
Assets:	£75,000
Liabilities:	£90,000

3 Comprehension/interpretation

3.1 By cutting back on management bonuses.
3.2 Turnover should increase at the same rate, profits even faster.
3.3 £50,000
3.4 Current creditors and bank.

4 Language focus

4.1 Asking questions – direct forms

1. Q: How much would you like to borrow?
2. Q: What is it for?
3. Q: Have you had more than one quotation?
4. Q: And are you asking for the full amount?
5. Q: How long a repayment term are you thinking of?
6. Q: Do you realise that the interest payments will be high?

7. Q: What sort of security arrangements are you offering?
8. Q: Can you remind me what sort of security we currently have?
9. Q: How much do you think they are worth?
10. Q: Is there anything else?

4.2   Questions – statement type

1. You'd like to extend your repayment period (wouldn't you)?
2. You haven't got any financial problems at the moment (have you)?
3. You see some improvement in your cash flow (don't you)?
4. You can offer some form of collateral (can't you)?
5. Your current liabilities are a bit higher than usual (aren't they)?
6. You intend to reduce your payment periods (don't you)?

5   Word Study

1. d   2. g   3. i   4. e   5. h   6. j   7. b   8. a   9. f   10. c

Section B: Management of working capital

Part 1: Types and uses of working capital

2   Reading

In Chart 2.2:

a.   Inventories
b.   Debtors
c.   Cash
d.   Raw materials
e.   Work in progress
f.   Finished goods
g.   Normal
h.   Abnormal requirements

3   Comprehension/interpretation

3.1   Extra money for emergencies, non-routine investments.
3.2   Obtain generous credit terms from suppliers.
      Give minimal credit to customers.

4   Language focus

4.1   Describing structures and systems

1. is divided
2. subdivided
3. former
4. latter
5. broken into

6. responsible
7. looks
8. Finally
9. split into
10. former
11. responsible
12. latter

4.2 Cause and effect

Over-stringent control can lead to disruption in production due to delays in raw materials. This may, in turn, result in the failure to meet customer orders and the subsequent loss of customer goodwill. This will inevitably mean a decline in sales which will cause costs to be controlled.

5 Word study

5.1

1. raised
2. rise
3. rise . . . raise
4. rose . . . raised

5.2

1. f   2. d   3. a   4. b   5. e   6. g   7. c

Part 2: Presenting a cash flow forecast

Listening tapescript

A: We've worked out the cash flow for the six months beginning June this year. As I've already mentioned, I plan to put in £30,000 of my own capital to start up the venture. As one would expect, the sales will not begin to picture until the second month, but after that they rise quite rapidly to reach £18,000 by the end of the six-month period.

B: And do you think this level of sales is sustainable over the winter?

A: Yes, certainly. In fact we hope to boost them further early next year.

B: Good. Anyway, I'm sorry. I interrupted you.

A: Right, on the cost side, the first month is going to prove a big drain. We have to start paying wages almost immediately at a rate of £6,000 per month. In the first month we need to buy in £3,000 worth of raw materials, although by the third month, August, that should settle down to about £1,000 per month. Other costs include the production and administrative overheads which I've set at £1,500 and £1,000 per month respectively.

B: Sorry to interrupt again. How accurate do you think those figures are?

A: Well, if anything, they're a little on the high side. We're obviously going to put quite a lot of effort into selling and distribution so I've set that at £1,800 per month – that includes advertising costs. It's difficult to forecast precisely but it should be round about that figure for each month. Then there's the rent on the factory. We've managed to get a very good deal – just £14,000 for the year with half of it payable at the beginning of June, the second half in December. Of course, we need to equip the plant and I've budgeted £20,000 outlay in the first month for machinery and equipment. Of course, that's a one-off payment and I don't anticipate further investment for at least a year. Certainly it should sustain production running at about £30,000 worth of monthly sales.

B: Sorry to interrupt again. Have you thought of leasing some of the equipment? That would spread the cost a bit.

A: Yes, we looked into that but with interest rates so high at the moment, we really feel that we're better off buying the stuff outright.

B: Fair enough.

A: So, that just leaves my own needs and as you can see I plan to take out £1,000 a month to keep body and soul together!

B: Are you sure that's enough?

A: Yes, I reckon we can just about manage on that. So, that means we've got closing cash balances rising to a peak of £31,700 negative in October. After that, our needs should come down quite rapidly so that I anticipate by the end of the six months we'll need a facility of around £22,000.

B: Well, thank you Mr Cairns. What you seem to be saying is that you would like a facility of over £30,000.

A: Yes, that's right. We'll keep you . . .

2 Listening

Chart 2.4

CASH FLOW FORECAST						
	June	July	August	Sept.	Oct.	Nov.
Opening cash balance		−11,300	−22,100	−29,400	−31,700	−28,000
Capital introduction	30,000					
Sales		2,000	5,000	10,000	15,000	18,000
Total receipts	30,000	2,000	5,000	10,000	15,000	18,000
Wages	6,000	6,000	6,000	6,000	6,000	6,000
Raw materials	3,000	1,500	1,000	1,000	1,000	1,000
Production overhead	1,500	1,500	1,500	1,500	1,500	1,500
Administrative overhead	1,000	1,000	1,000	1,000	1,000	1,000
Selling and distrib.	1,800	1,800	1,800	1,800	1,800	1,800
Factory rent	7,000					
Equipment and machinery	20,000					
Drawings	1,000	1,000	1,000	1,000	1,000	1,000
Total payments	41,300	12,800	12,300	12,300	12,300	12,300
Movement in cash	−11,300	−10,800	−7,300	−2,300	+3,700	+5,700
Closing cash balance	**−11,300**	**−22,100**	**−29,400**	**−31,700**	**−28,000**	**−22,300**

3   Comprehension/interpretation

3.1   Because customers will normally be allowed 30 days credit.
3.2   No, he feels they are probably overstated.
3.3   No, it's a good deal.
3.4   Interest rates too high.

4   Language focus

4.1   Future reference – forecasting

A: When are you planning to open the factory?
B: We reckon it will open at the beginning of July.
A: In the meantime, are you going to promote your product?
B: No, we hope to start selling in July.
A: So you don't expect any orders in July?
B: Probably not, we anticipate orders will come in from August onwards.
A: What level of sales do you forecast for August?
B: Well, we project sales of about £20,000.
A: That sounds very optimistic. Do you have the figures to support that?
B: No, not on me. We are going to inform all prospective customers by direct mail and we are confident of £20,000 sales as an early result.
A: The effect of direct mail is notoriously difficult to predict. Are you going to do anything else?
B: Yes, we are going to telephone all major users in the industry and arrange appointments.

4.2   Scale of likelihood

1.   We are unlikely to achieve sales of more than £30,000.
2.   We could lease equipment but interest rates are very high.
3.   We can't reduce costs below this level.
4.   There's a good chance we will need an overdraft of £32,000.
5.   Sales are likely to rise in the second half of the year.
6.   I will only take a salary of £1,000 a month.
7.   We should be ready to start production next month.
8.   There could/might be some difficulties in production at the start.

5   Word study

To work out the figures.
To put in your own money.
To start up a business.
To buy in raw materials.
To settle on a low figure.
To set up.
To put effort into sales.
To be better off.
To take out the profits.
To manage on a low salary.

UNIT 3
Financial measurements

Section A: The profit and loss account

Part 1: Reading a profit and loss account

2 Reading

Chart 3.1

CONSOLIDATED PROFIT AND LOSS ACCOUNT		
	Year ended 31 December	
	1991	1990
	£000	£000
Turnover	65,000	60,000
Direct costs	(30,000)	(29,000)
Gross profit	35,000	31,000
Fixed costs	(15,500)	(14,800)
Operating profit	19,500	16,200
Minority shareholders	(5,400)	(4,800)
Profit before tax	14,100	11,400
Tax	(1,800)	(1,900)
Profit after tax	12,300	9,500
Extraordinary item	(450)	
Net profit	11,850	9,500
Preference shareholders' dividend	(50)	(40)
Ordinary shareholders' dividend	(300)	(190)
Retained earnings	11,500	9,280
Earnings per share	31p	25p

3 Comprehension/interpretation

3.1 Up to you!

3.2 Non-attributable overheads such as administrative costs, power etc.

3.3 One-off costs not incurred in the day-to-day running of the business.

3.4 Preference shareholders receive a fixed, guaranteed dividend; ordinary shareholders' dividend depends on the results.

3.5 Because this key ratio (the yield) tells us what sort of rate of return an investor can expect.

4   Language focus

4.1   Defining and non-defining clauses

1. The profit and loss statement, (which) you received yesterday, makes depressing reading.
2. The bookkeeper (whom) we hired last year made some terrible mistakes.
3. The attached accounts were audited two months late.
4. The production manager who was fired two days ago underestimated the operating costs.
5. Profits, which were well down on last year, have still not been distributed to the employees.

4.2   Passive versus active voice

1. The profitability of the company is summarised by/in the profit and loss account.
2. £1.8 million in tax is paid by this company.
3. A fixed dividend of 50,000 was received by the preference shareholders.
4. The company retains earnings of £11.5 million.
5. The taxable profit is calculated by the accountants.
6. Investing in property has incurred considerable costs.
7. Profits will be maximised by deferring taxation.
8. Reducing production capacity would have made savings.

5   Word study

Verb	Noun	Adjective
to operate	operation	operational
to deduct	deduction	deductible
to tax	tax/taxation	taxable
to apply	application	applicable
to contribute	contribution	
to retain	retention	
to distribute	distribution	

Part 2: Profit and cash flow

Listening tapescript

Pete: We've had a look at the profitability side and we both seem to agree that this year's Profit & Loss Account looks very healthy on the face of it. However, we have continued to have serious cash flow problems and we've got to do something about it. In my opinion, the fundamental problem is our deferred terms of payment – we've still got too big a gap – about 60 days – between paying our suppliers and receiving payment for sales.

Simon: Yes, that's probably true but I feel there are other underlying problems. One is the asset side of our business – our recent cash flow crisis is particularly due to sudden investment in information technology. Our profitability in a way has been kept artificially high by very low depreciation over the last few years. Now, we can't afford not to invest and its draining our cash resources.

Pete: I think you're exaggerating Simon. Depreciation will reduce our profits more during the next couple of years but not to a significant extent. No, in my opinion we're still under-capitalised and we've been over-trading this last year.

Simon: I can't agree with you. Our turnover has increased substantially but our margins have improved dramatically. We've controlled our costs and we've worked hard in the Sales Department to improve our credit control. No, in my view, we are not planning well enough. Look at the crisis we had a few months ago when we received the massive tax bill. I'd like to know why we hadn't retained sufficient funds to pay it. Why did it come as such a shock?

Pete: It didn't come as a shock. It's quite simple. We did retain for tax, but the retention was soaked up as working capital to help fund the sort of growth we've had over the last six months.

Simon: That's exactly my point. No financial planning!

Pete: I resent that. In the circumstances, I think my department is doing its best to . . .

2 Listening

Chart 3.3

Problems	Pete	Simon
Credit terms	✓	✓
Investment planning		✓
Under-capitalisation	✓	
Over-trading	✓	
Financial planning		✓

3 Comprehension/interpretation

3.1 Information technology.

3.2 Very little investment.

3.3 Costs and credit have been controlled.

3.4 Soaked up by working capital.

4 Language focus

4.1 Opinion-giving

1. N   2. N   3. S   4. W   5. N   6. S   7. N   8. W   9. S   10. S

4.2 Agreeing and disagreeing

1. c   2. f   3. e   4. a   5. b   6. h   7. d   8. g

5 Word study

Depth of problem	Size of problem	Importance of problem	Timing
fundamental	substantial	insignificant	immediate
underlying	massive	irrelevant	sudden
superficial	huge	noticeable	instant
	tiny	marked	
	enormous	significant	

Section B: The balance sheet

Part 1: Explaining the balance sheet

2 Reading

Chart 3.4

BALANCE SHEET				
as at 31 December		1991		1990
		£000		£000
Fixed assets				
Intangibles		1,500		1,400
Tangibles		7,500		7,200
		9,000		8,600
Current assets				
Stocks	3,200		2,800	
Debtors	1,300		1,400	
Cash	350		250	
	4,850		4,450	
Current liabilities				
Creditors	(2,200)		(2,100)	
Current assets less		2,650		2,350
current liabilities				
Total assets less		11,650		10,950
current liabilities				
Long-term loans		(2,450)		(2,850)
Deferred taxation		(450)		
Net assets		8,750		8,100
Capital and reserves				
Share capital		6,500		6,500
Share premium account		1,400		1,200
Revaluation of fixed assets		1,150		800
Retained profit		(300)		(400)
Shareholders' funds		**8,750**		**8,100**

3 Comprehension/interpretation

3.1 For assessing the real value in cases of takeover, liquidation, etc.

3.2 Because assessment and collection of taxes is often carried out retrospectively.

3.3 To take account of the difference between issued share value and the actual price of the shares.

---

4 Language focus

4.1 Prepositions – amount and difference

1. When current liabilities are subtracted from current assets, there is a net balance of £50,000.
2. Debtors have increased from last year's figure of £25,000 to a total of £48,000.
3. Our bank loan has decreased by 10 per cent so a balance of £25,000 remains.
4. The bank overdraft stood at £18,000 last year. It has been reduced by £5,000 and now stands at £13,000.
5. There has been an increase of 2 per cent per year in interest payments. So in fact it's rocketed from 6 per cent in 1987 to 12 per cent this year.

4.2 Sequence

1. d   2. g   3. a   4. e   5. b   6. h   7. c   8. f

5 Word study

1. is valued
2. is set aside
3. was topped up
4. are set at a book value . . . are worth
5. is charged

Part 2: Valuing goodwill

Listening tapescript

A: I think you all know that we've had an approach from Technics plc. They've expressed a strong interest in buying the firm. We've already agreed that we're interested in pursuing their approach, so today we have to discuss the sort of price we aim to get. John, you're here to advise us on the financial side, would you like to say a few words?

B: Yes, of course. Essentially we need to look at two figures when trying to value the firm. The first is the asset value of the firm, and the second is the earnings potential of the firm. Technics will be looking for a good return on their capital investment and they'll also be looking for high profit potential on top. I think there's no doubt that your firm is extremely attractive – it's highly profitable, has an excellent reputation and a sound financial base. Right, on the assets side, your latest balance sheet puts the net assets at £176,000. Of course, your major fixed asset is the property but you've got £290,000 owing on a secured loan and further amounts of £56,000 for accrued interest and of course £80,000 for the distance learning equipment which you've been investing in. Really, to sum up, I don't think Technics are going to buy you for your asset value. We should aim to get the current figure, certainly, and this will cover all the partners' undrawn profits and capital investment. No, what Technics are interested in is your name, your reputation and your earning potential. Your average profits over the last three years have been about £50,000 on a turnover of about £400,000 – that's not brilliant but if we look at your gross margins they are in the region of 30 to 40 per cent. This is what we should aim to sell and I think we should be looking for a goodwill figure of about £500,000 which represents ten years of net profits or three years of gross profits. So, before I go on, are there any questions?

2 Listening

Chart 3.6

Assets	Net asset value	Long-term liabilities		Target price
	£176,000	£290,000; £56,000; £80,000		£176,000
Earnings	Average profits	Average turnover	Gross margin	Target price
(goodwill)	£50,000	£400,00	30–40%	£500,000

3 Comprehension/interpretation

3.1 Because the firm is highly profitable.
3.2 They will be soaked up by long-term liabilities.
3.3 Undrawn profits and capital investment.
3.4 Yes.

4 Language focus

4.1 Continuous forms

1. We will be making a profit of £100,000 this year.
2. We should be investing in time share deals.
4. They have been losing money continuously.
6. We were recruiting salespeople throughout the year.
7. He's always talking about things; he never does them.
10. He has been acquiring companies all his life.

4.2 Verb + preposition: **to look . . .**

1. If you *look at* your current figures, they don't make happy reading.
2. We've taken on a consultant. She's going to *look at/into* our supply chain.
3. You shouldn't *look up to* consultants. They make mistakes like the rest of us.
4. We've been *looking for* a new bookkeeper for weeks; maybe we need to advertise nationally.
5. I *looked up* the telephone number in the directory.
6. Finance managers should never look down on other departmental managers just because they don't understand finance.
7. We're *looking into* the possibility of subcontracting some of the production. It looks as if it may be possible.
8. If you *look after* the pennies, the pounds will take care of themselves.

5 Word study (tapescript)

1. 1.99 million
2. 201,400
3. 99
4. 5.986
5. 500,000
6. 12⅞
7. 503
8. 1,499,000
9. 370 days
10. 8.015

Suggested answers:

1. Just about/nearly 2 million
2. Just over 200,000
3. Just below 100
4. A little below 6
5. Precisely 500,000
6. Nearly 13
7. Just over 500
8. Nearly 1,500,000
9. Around 400 days
10. About 8

UNIT 4
Financial analysis

Section A: Ratio analysis

Part 1: Ratio analysis

2 *Reading*

Chart 4.1

Key indicators	Ratios used	Interpretation
Liquidity	(i) Current ratio (ii) Quick ratio	More current assets than liabilities = healthy Takes into account stock levels
Capital structure	(i) Gearing (ii) Income gearing	Ability to meet long-term debt High borrowing indicates vulnerability to interest rate rise
Efficiency	(i) Sales/stock (ii) Average collection period	Can see how fast stock is turned over Debtors versus sales per day
Profitability	(i) Profit margin (ii) Return on capital (iii) Return on owner's equity	Operational profitability Use of company assets Important for share price

3 *Comprehension/interpretation*

(The answers are very much open for discussion. Below are some suggestions.)

3.1 Return on owner's equity
3.2 Efficiency ratios
3.3 Profit margin
3.4 Collection period
3.5 Capital structure and profitability

4 Language focus

4.1 Adjective modification

1. unusually high
2. highly geared
3. particularly short
4. dangerously long
5. considerably slower

4.2 Adjectives and adverbs

Noun	Adjective	Adverb
profitability	profitable	profitably
efficiency	efficient	efficiently
health	healthy	healthily
appropriacy	appropriate	appropriately
operation	operational	operationally
finance	financial	financially
productivity	productive	productively
management	managerial	managerially

5 Word study

5.1

Positive	Average/okay	Negative
healthy	reasonable	disastrous
strong	adequate	weak
excellent	satisfactory	vulnerable
tremendous	moderate	poor
marvellous		disappointing
		catastrophic

5.2

1. All except *strong*, *weak*, *vulnerable*.
2. All can be used.

Part 2: Business analysis

Listening tapescript

(FM = finance manager; MM = marketing manager)

FM: Well, I'm very interested in hearing your views on investment over the next three years.

MM: Good. So let me start by reviewing where we stand. We're operating in three major sectors of consultancy work – those are financial, personnel and strategic consulting. My estimate is that we currently hold about 10 per cent of the financial consultancy market share, 20 per cent of the personnel sector, and just 5 per cent in strategic consulting.

FM: I thought we were planning to move into IT – information technology?

MM: We were, but there are some very big competitors out there and we've decided to build on our strengths instead.

FM: Fair enough. Go on.

MM: Now these three sectors are growing at different rates – the financial sector is pretty static, the human resources is expanding rapidly and strategic consultancy is moving slowly.

FM: And what about margins in these three areas?

MM: I thought you'd ask that. I was just coming to it. Before I do, your department's just let me have the latest sales figures for the three areas and they are pretty much in line with market trends. Turnover in financial consultancy is up by 4 per cent, personnel has increased by 25 per cent and strategic work is up by 5 per cent. Now, on the profit side, it's rather a different picture in terms of margins though not total profit. The personnel sector contributes most in total but the strategic consultancy has by far the best margins – we are often working on 300 to 400 per cent, whereas on areas like recruitment consultancy, we normally work on around 50 per cent.

FM: Yes, that fits in with your latest batch of sales figures. So what do you feel is the right direction?

MM: I was just coming to that. Before I do, let me just add that the margins on financial consultancy are around 40 per cent. So, now on to the investment. I think we should split our investment between personnel and strategic work. I would suggest allocating about 25 per cent of the budget for new projects in the strategic consultancy group, 40 per cent of the budget to personnel and the remaining 35 per cent on advertising and public relations for all three sectors.

FM: So, nothing for financial consulting?

MM: No, nothing specific. I reckon we can maintain our market share without any new project development.

2 Listening

Chart 4.2

Sectors of business	Market share (%)	Market growth	Turnover increase (%)	Profits (%)	Investment (%)
Financial	10	Static	4	40	
Personnel	20	Expanding rapidly	25	50	40 } 35
Strategic	5	Moving slowly	5	300–400	25

3 Comprehension/interpretation

Up to you!

4 Language focus

4.1 Present continuous

2. The human resource sector is expanding rapidly at the moment.
4. We are gaining market share in the present climate.
6. What is he doing? – He is telephoning America.
8. I am waiting for the results of the survey. Then I will decide.

4.2 Presentations – linkers

1. j   2. e   3. a   4. f   5. i   6. g   7. b   8. c   9. h   10. d

5 Word study

1. f   2. g   3. a   4. l   5. i   6. j   7. e   8. k   9. b   10. h   11. c   12. d

Section B: Financial evaluation

Part 1: Capital investment budgeting

2 Reading

a. 932   b. 0

3 Comprehension/interpretation

3.1 Recoup after 3 years / too simple / need 5 year view / doesn't take account of opportunity cost.
3.2 Full 5 years / does not take account of time value of money.
3.3 Future earnings are translated into present value / rather complex.

4 Language focus

4.1 Conditions

1. If the project fails, we will lose a lot of money.
2. We can extend the payback period if we adopt an ARR method.
3. We will get a truer picture if we take into account present values of money.
4. We won't invest unless we foresee a realistic chance of long-term profits.
5. As long as the project is financed from outside sources, we (will) have to ensure a much higher rate of return.
6. If we lose money in the first two years, we will start to doubt the viability of the project.
7. Unless we are committed to the project long-term, we won't carry it through.
8. Breakeven point will come a year earlier if we manage to reach these sales targets.

4.2 Report-writing

1. This report aims to evaluate the return on investment
2. A more complex view of the project must be taken.
3. If the ARR method is adopted, the cash flow can be spread.
4. A DCF method has therefore been applied.
5. The DCF has been set at two different rates.
6. This means an internal rate of return of 18% can probably be expected.
7. It can be concluded that the 25% DCF is unrealistic.
8. Given the activities of our competitors, it is recommended that the project is adopted.

5 Word study

1. b   2. d   3. a   4. e   5. c

Part 2: Costing and pricing a new product

Listening tapescript

A: So can we all agree about the facts? The direct cost on AX21 has been calculated at £4.50 per unit and the fixed costs – that's for overheads – have been set at £2.50, giving us a total cost of £7 per unit?

B: Well, those figures have been worked out at a production of 2,500 units per month. I'm not sure how accurate that figure is.

C: We've been through all this before. We feel that's a fair average based on projected sales figures for the first year.

B: Yes, I know that, but what if we achieve higher sales through a lower retail price?

C: Well, that's what we're here today to discuss.

A: That's right. Now a typical mark-up for this type of product would be around 25 per cent from the manufacturer and then a further 30 per cent for the retailer. So that would give us a retail price in the shops of around £11.40. How does that compare with our competitors?

C: Well, we've got two major competitors in this class of product – Phiso is retailing their machine at £10 per unit while Safto is at a slightly higher price at £12. I feel we should go in at a higher price than our competitors – the product is certainly more up-to-date and more stylish.

A: If we set a market price of around £13, what would that do to sales?

B: Our research shows that demand is very elastic – in other words very responsive to price. We might well lose out on volume. The production line has been prepared for 2,500 units per month, so a drop in the production figure will mean a corresponding rise in costs per unit.

A: So, we should aim initially at reaching our target. That seems to me a question of pitching just above the competitor's price – say £12.50. At this price, we'll get very good margins and so will our retailers.

B: I think that's too high. If we lost sales through too high a price, it would jeopardise the whole project. I'm inclined to be more conservative and come in just below Safto's price – say £11.50. At that price we would still protect our margins and be pretty sure of reaching our sales targets.

A: All right, let's set the recommended retail price at £12.50 but come in with a promotional offer which discounts that price by a pound. That way we give ourselves the flexibility to push the price up if we feel the market can bear it.

2 Listening

In Chart 4.4:

a. £12.50
b. £11.50
c. £ 8.75 (1.75 = 25%)
d. £ 7.00 (2.50)
e. £ 4.50

3 Comprehension/interpretation

3.1 Direct costs can be attributed to units of production, fixed costs do not vary according to production.
3.2 Up to you!
3.3 Because the fixed costs are spread over fewer units.
3.4 It appears to the consumer as a bargain.

4 Language focus

4.1 Conditionals I and II

1. If we set a market price of £13, what will/would that do to sales?
2. We would still protect our margins if we fixed a price of £11.50.
3. If the market could bear it, we would be able to push the price up.
4. We would lose market share if our competitor dropped its price.
5. I would resign if I won the lottery.
6. Unless there is a price war, we will make a good profit.
7. If production falls, our unit costs will go up.
8. We won't offer a discount if the retailers are prepared to limit their margins.

4.2 Verb + preposition

1. We compared our prices to our competitors'.
2. Do you agree with Peter?
3. They agreed on the project and signed the contract.
4. These figures have been worked out by our accountants.
5. Sales are likely to respond quickly to changes in price.
6. If we push up the price, sales might come down.
7. Are you prepared for the price war?
8. We aimed at a lower price than our competitors.
9. We set the price at £12.50.
10. We prevented the competitors from gaining market share.

5 Word study

1. f   2. h   3. j   4. a   5. i   6. k   7. d   8. c   9. g   10. b

UNIT 5
Standards and compliance

Section A: *Standardising financial reporting on a European basis*

Part 1: Comparability of accounts

2 *Reading*

In Chart 5.1:

a. ($28m)
b. $285m
c. $6.6bn (77)
d. $3.3bn (197)
e. $3bn (151)
f. $2bn (79)

3 *Comprehension/interpretation*

3.1 Because the market cannot compare companies competing for capital.
3.2 $76m resulting from insurance claims.
3.3 Nearly £100m in severance pay costs.
3.4 By writing off discounts in bonds ($7m).
3.5 Revenue tonne kilometres.
3.6 (i) Different methods of valuation.
     (ii) Some aircraft are not shown (e.g. leased aircraft).
3.7 Because the US makes the following changes:
     (i) adds $680m in goodwill value
     (ii) deducts $575m for historical costing of fleet
     (iii) deducts $233 for deferred taxes

4 *Language focus*

4.1 Connectors

1. Despite having to set aside £20m for redundancies, the company showed a profit.
2. Although the company showed a profit, the balance sheet looks increasingly fragile.
3. American companies must add goodwill values to shareholders' funds whereas British companies can simply write them off.
4. We made an overall loss even though our American operations were highly profitable.
5. The industry has its own methods of analysing performance. However, analysts need to be able to evaluate comparable accounts.

4.2   Subordinate clauses

2. which suggests that the provision was made simply
to take advantage of this tax concession
3. which were issued during the year
4. who hopes to arrive at its true profits
5. which presents the IASC with the difficult task . . .
6. which is/are shown in different company accounts
7. which are operated by different airlines
8. which makes it still more difficult to compare airlines

5   *Word study*

to tighten up standards
to arise from insurance claims
to amount to $20 million
to set aside $60 million for taxation
to take advantage of a tax concession
to write off a bad debt
to spread over ten years
to translate into dollars
to be recorded at $20 million
to account for depreciation
to apply to cost calculations
to keep out of the accounts
to bring into the accounts
to knock off the value
to take away from the profits

Part 2: Analysing performance

Listening tapescript

A: I had a terrible trip over. Just about every flight was delayed.
B: I'm sorry. Mind you, that seems to be the case more and more.
C: Okay, let's get started. Now we've got a full agenda today. Has everybody seen a
copy?
[murmur 'yes']
C: Good, everybody happy with it? Okay, let's get started straight away with item 1 –
that's our topical comparison. This week we've chosen two go-ahead high-tech
companies – Saxon and Pixbury. They've both been hitting the headlines of the
business pages quite a lot recently and I know we've had a number of enquiries from
our regular investors. So, John, would you like to put us in the picture?
B: Sure. Well I've been looking at their most recent published accounts and I'll go
through some key figures. On the face of it, Saxon performed much better than
Pixbury last year. Net income was well up on the previous year – a total of
$202 million – whereas Pixbury announced just $55 million profit for the year. However, as usual, it's worth looking a bit more closely at the figures. Pixbury accounted
for $45 million in development costs – while Saxon only posted $6 million – now either

Saxon is resting on its laurels or it's applying a different accounting convention – I suspect the latter.

C: Why's that John?

B: Well I know they've both been working on some new electronic sensor systems for environmental projects. Both have filed patents; in fact Saxon made the asset side of their balance sheet look very healthy by putting down $195 million as intangibles – representing the future value of their patents – while Pixbury have a much more modest figure – just $22 million.

C: So, if I understand you correctly, you're saying Saxon's profit figures are artificially high – maybe by as much as $40 million.

B: Well, not necessarily. You could argue that Pixbury's are much too low because they haven't spread development costs over the life of the products they are working on.

C: Right. I see what you're getting at. Anything further to add?

B: Yes, there are a couple of other things I'd like to mention. Pixbury have knocked $2 million off their profits for the discount they offered on a bond issue last year – again I'd have expected them to spread that as a financing cost over a number of years.

A: Yes, that's normal practice, isn't it?

B: Certainly in the UK. Finally, I'd like to draw your attention to the acquisition Saxon made during last year – that was Britmax International. Now they've written off just $1.5 million in goodwill against their reserves, while I know for a fact that goodwill was valued much higher than that – more like $24 million.

D: Yes, but surely they'll spread it over at least five years against future profits. What have they added to their equity for the acquisiton?

B: Well, that's not clear unfortunately. My calculation is about $47 million, which seems realistic.

C: Okay John, thanks. Could you just sum up?

B: Well, my feeling is that Pixbury is the better bet long term. Saxon have produced some very impressive results but I favour the more cautious approach adopted by Pixbury.

C: Right, thanks John. Let's leave that and move on to the next item.

2 Listening

Chart 5.2

	Saxon	Pixbury
Development costs	S6m	S45m
Bond issue		S2m
Net income	S202m	S55m
Assets: equity	+47m	
intangibles	195m	22m

3 Comprehension/interpretation

3.1 Up to you!

3.2 Up to you!

4   Language focus

4.1   Meetings

1. d   2. h   3. j   4. a   5. e   6. g   7. b   8. f   9. c   10. i

4.2   Degree – modification of adjectives

1. S   2. N   3. W   4. S   5. S   6. N   7. W   8. S   9. W   10. S

5   Word study

Forward-looking companies	Technology	Asset base	Reporting policy
dynamic	state-of-the-art	healthy	modest
thrusting	leading edge	strong	conservative
go-ahead	advanced	robust	low-key
enterprising	high-tech	substantial	cautious
	modern		

Section B: The role of auditors

Part 1: The role of auditors

2   Reading

1. T   2. T   3. F   4. F   5. F   6. T

3   Comprehension/interpretation

3.1   1. a   2. c   3. b
3.2   If senior managers or directors are involved with the fraud.
3.3   Companies operating in the financial sector.
3.4   A case of bankruptcy where investors lost a lot of money.
3.5   Up to you!

4   Language focus

4.1   Mass and units

1. U   2. U   3. U   4. U   5. U   6. U   7. U   8. U   9. U   10. C   11. C
12. C   13. U   14. U

4.2   Obligation

1. You must/have to obey the law
2. You don't have to report fraud.
3. You should report fraud.
4. You must/have to respect a client's confidence.
5. You should follow the code.
6. You mustn't be employed by a client.

5 Word study

1. f   2. e   3. g   4. h   5. i   6. d   7. c   8. l   9. j   10. b   11. a   12. k

Part 2: Ethics in accounting

Listening tapescript

A: Okay, there are a couple of issues I'd like to bring up. Firstly there's the old chestnut of your fixed assets. We let it go last year but we really can't in all fairness continue valuing some of these at historical cost – it just doesn't give an accurate picture.

B: True, but we'd be a much bigger target for takeover if we were to publish real values.

A: Maybe, but besides the outside world, you owe it to your shareholders to present a more honest picture of the real value of the company.

B: I suppose you're right. No doubt you're talking mainly about the freehold property?

A: Yes, you've got it down at £2.2 million. What do you think it's really worth?

B: At least £5 million. So, I'll get on to the estate manager and get him to arrange an independent valuation.

A: Good, let me have the report as soon as you have it.

B: I will.

A: Right, there's another issue. On the liabilities side. I'd like to talk about this extra-ordinary item – £500,000 – which you've set aside for redundancy payments resulting from the closure of the Plymouth plant. How accurate is this figure?

B: Well, of course it's not exact. It could well be considerably higher – it depends on the number of early retirements we manage to agree.

A: So you're planning to finance those out of your existing pension fund?

B: Yes, that's right. It should cover that side. Another factor is how many of the work-force we can persuade to move up to work in the plant in Scotland.

A: What's the likely figure?

B: If we're lucky it could be 20 per cent of the planned redundancies – and that would mean £500,000 would cover those that have to leave.

A. What's your worst case?

B: It might go as high as £1 million.

A: Really, then I think we should set aside at least £750,000 as a more realistic figure.

B: We really can't do that. It's political you see. The more we put in the accounts, the more the unions are going to push for.

A: I see. Right, so you want to stick to half a million?

B: Yes, that's the board's decision.

2 Listening

In Chart 5.3

a.   £2.2m   c.   at least £5m
b.   £500,000   d.   £750,000

3 Comprehension/interpretation

3.1 It makes the company a bigger target for takeover.
3.2 It would present a more honest picture for shareholders.
3.3 Redundancy payments.
3.4 No.
3.5 Because he fears the trade unions will use it as an argument for higher payments.

4 Language focus

4.1 Short responses

1. h   2. i   3. f   4. b   5. g   6. d   7. a   8. c   9. e

4.2 Meetings – controlling and structuring

1. d   2. g   3. a   4. i   5. b   6. e   7. c   8. f   9. h

5 Word study

honest	independent	relevant	prudent	consistent
fair	disinterested	suitable	safe	reliable
true	impartial	applicable	cautious	logical
accurate	objective	appropriate	modest	steady
representative	unbiased		conservative	rational

6 Transfer

1. e   2. d   3. g   4. b   5. h   6. a   7. f   8. c   9. j   10. i

UNIT 6
Taxation

Section A: Corporate and personal taxation

Part 1: Introduction to corporate taxation

2 *Reading*

In Chart 6.1:

a. Marginal ▨

b. Average ▦

In Chart 6.2:

a. Cost by FIFO method
b. Cost by LIFO method
c. Cost by average-cost method

3 *Comprehension/interpretation*

3.1 Because it is taxed only once as an extension of its owners.
3.2 As income earned (corporation tax) and as a dividend (personal income tax).
3.3 Because most investors will be paying this rate.
3.4 Five years (business equipment).
3.5 Because prices have consistently been rising and this means the company can charge more to costs in the present.

4 *Language focus*

4.1 Expressing comparative relations

1. The higher the price, the lower the profit.
    The lower the price, the higher the profit.
2. The longer we wait, the higher the ROI.
    The shorter the time, the lower the ROI.
3. The lower the target, the more probable it is.
    The higher the target, the less probable it is.
4. The higher the demand, the greater the trade deficit.
    The lower the demand, the smaller the trade deficit.

4.2 Much/many/few/little

1. Few people realise how much tax they could avoid paying if they studied the tax laws.
2. Many people believe they pay too much tax.
3. There is too little time and too many problems to talk about irrelevant issues.
4. There isn't much evidence to support these figures.
5. You'll pay much less tax in the Cayman Islands than most places.
6. Very few tax authorities have clear plans for corporation tax in the future.
7. There are many fewer opportunities to avoid tax nowadays.
8. Few companies operate the FIFO method nowadays.

5 Word study

Verb	Noun	Adjective
to govern	government	governable
to provide	provision	provisional
to decide	decision	decisive
to consider	consideration	considerable
to apply	application	applicable
to depreciate	depreciation	depreciable
to deduct	deduction	deductible
to assess	assessment	assessible
to sacrifice	sacrifice	sacrificial
to profit	profit	profitable

6 Transfer

B: Prepare a presentation on current inventory calculations/methods. Give this explanation to your partner.

Part 2: Briefing on personal taxation

Listening tapescript

A: As part of your briefing on UK location decisions, we've asked Geoff Peters, Chief Inspector of Taxes at the Inland Revenue, to give you a short overview of personal taxation as it stands at the moment. Right, I'll hand you straight over to Geoff.

B: Good afternoon, ladies and gentlemen. Unfortunately, in the UK too, there's no getting away from the man you all love to hate – the taxman. Now, I'm going to keep this brief and to the point; I'll leave the details to the discussion afterwards and try to answer any specific questions you may have at the end. What I'd like to do essentially is to answer two questions. Firstly, how is personal taxation structured in the UK? And secondly, how is it levied?

So, if you take a look at this transparency, you'll see that, contrary to popular opinion, UK personal taxation is both simple and relatively low. There are two rates: 25 per cent on taxable income up to £23,700, and 40 per cent on income above this figure. You'll notice I say taxable income, as, like most countries, there are a series of deductions and allowances which can be taken into account before arriving at your net taxable income figure. The major one relates to the status of the individual: a single person's allowance at present stands at £3,295, while a married person's allowance is currently £5,015.

At this point I should mention that the government has recently introduced legislation which allows married couples to opt for separate taxation.

Other allowances or deductions which are common are, firstly, tax relief on private pensions. At the moment this is allowable up to 17.5 per cent of total income, up to the age of 35, rising to 40 per cent above 60 years old. Also the much vaunted tax relief on mortgages or loans to buy a house – here there is currently 7 per cent tax relief on the interest payable to the bank or building society up to a maximum of £30,000 capital borrowed. The percentage relief obviously depends on the interest rates that are operative at any one time.

Right, that covers the first part of my presentation, I'd now like to move on to how personal tax is levied. The Inland Revenue obliges employers to operate a PAYE (Pay As You Earn) scheme, which means the tax is deductible at source. In other words, by the employer before making out the monthly salary cheque or bank transfer to the employee. The tax is then collected direct from the employer. At the same time I should mention that the employer is obliged to deduct National Insurance from the employee's salary – the employee's contribution being roughly 9 per cent of income, the employer's ranging from 5 to 10 per cent. These are approximate figures as it is also income-related. This last transparency summarises the situation.

Right, ladies and gentlemen, that covers the broad picture. I'm sure you'd like to ask me for some specific details.

2 Listening

In Charts 6.4 and 6.5:

a. 25%
b. 40%
c. 3,295
d. 5,015
e. 17½% to 40%
f. 7%
g. PAYE
h. 9
i. 5–10

3 Comprehension/interpretation

3.1 Part 1: How is personal tax structured?
    Part 2: How is it levied?
3.2 It is complex and high.
3.3 Married couples can opt for separate taxation.
3.4 Social security (pensions, health, benefits).

4 Language focus

4.1 Presentation

INTRODUCTION
1. c   2. d   3. a   4. b

MAIN PART
1. e   2. f   3. a   4. c   5. g   6. d   7. b   8. h

CONCLUSION
1. d   2. c   3. a   4. b

5 Word study

1. e   2. a   3. g   4. h   5. l   6. j   7. c   8. b   9. d   10. f   11. i   12. k

Section B: Harmonising taxation in Europe

Part 1: Tax harmonisation in Europe

2 Reading

Chart 6.7

Location	Relative tax rates (corporation and personal tax) Build flexibility into business plans Tax incentives (e.g. Ireland and Belgium)
Pricing	Range of possible prices – review prices every three years Adequate documentation justifying transfer prices Pricing intangible items – locate intangibles in low-tax areas
Financial structure	Interest charges deductible, dividends are not – gear up in high tax areas, keep equity low in low-tax areas (thin capitalisation) Stick on gearing of 3 : 1

3 Comprehension/interpretation

3.1 Competition between countries for inward investment.
3.2 Ireland and Belgium.
3.3 Brands, marketing and distribution.
3.4 Paying low taxes on interest-earning equity.

4 Language focus

4.1 Noun compounds

1. Well-prepared and informative documentation.
2. A well-qualified German tax consultant.
3. A highly-profitable Swiss watch manufacturer.
4. Rapidly-growing unfair competition.
5. Unequally aligned European tax rates.

4.2 Similarity and difference

1. Like many major European cities, London is an expensive place to live.
2. Inventory levels were as forecast.
3. Although they have much in common, they differ in vital ways; for example the two companies have a totally different structure.
4. There is a tremendous variety of tax incentives. However, in one sense, they are similar to each other in that they are all difficult to understand.
5. In the UK we all pay the same rate of corporation tax; unlike in Germany where rates vary from 35 to 56 per cent.

5 Word study

1. f 2. i 3. d 4. k 5. b 6. l 7. g 8. c 9. a 10. e 11. h 12. j

Part 2: Plant location decisions

Listening tapescript

A: Right, ladies and gentlemen, I suggest we get down to business. As you know, the most important item on our agenda today is the location of the new plant. Susan will bring you up to date with our latest thinking. Susan . . .

B: Thank you. Well, I'll be brief. We've narrowed down the decision to three locations. Scotland, just outside Edinburgh; France, near our existing distribution centre in Lyon, and thirdly Germany, in the south near Nuremburg. I'd like to outline the factors that I feel should be taken into account when coming to our final decision. To help us to see this clearly I've prepared a transparency. Now, as you can see, I've broken down these factors along the top here.

First of all, arguably the most vital in terms of efficiency of our whole operation, I've put communications – meaning the ease of supply and delivery from and to the European market and internal information systems. As you can see, Lyon in its central European position scores highest in this area, with Scotland coming off worst. We'll have to come back to this point to discuss it in more detail as it is crucial to our future.

The second factor is the labour force. Here there are really two considerations: firstly availability and secondly skill. Scotland comes out on top with a relatively high unemployment figure and a good skill base. There is little to choose between France and Germany.

The third factor is plant construction cost, i.e. the initial investment cost. Again Scotland comes out best with slightly lower costs, mainly due to lower labour costs and cheaper land prices. France is weighted a little higher in terms of investment costs while Germany is very much higher. These last two factors are of course contributing factors to manufacturing costs – here again we see a slight advantage gained by Scotland with Lyon very close behind and Germany lagging behind in third place.

So that brings me to the final factor, which is also the most complex . . .

C: Just before you move onto tax, can I ask you about the plant construction?
B: Of course, go ahead.
C: I was wondering whether any of the countries we are considering offered any help with investment costs?
B: That's a good question and one which I have taken into account when weighting tax benefits, so if I may go on?
C: Please.
B: Right, as I was saying, tax is rather more complex. It's not just a question of comparing corporate tax rates in the different locations – on this basis Scotland comes out slightly ahead of France and a long way ahead of Germany. It's a question of looking at the whole incentive package. Now Scotland provides tax relief on property investment when employment is offered – this is one of the reasons the plant construction costs are lower than the others. On the other hand, France has a very attractive package over the first five years of operation which means that we virtually pay no tax on profits during these initial years.
D: Can I interrupt?
B: Please do.
D: Did you take this into account when setting manufacturing costs?
B: No, I've excluded tax relief on running costs and profits.
D: I don't see how you can do that. You've just said that in Scotland the tax relief was taken into account when calculating plant construction costs.
B: That's true but that's a fixed initial cost. I felt it was better to include it in that calculation but exclude other tax benefits so we could consider them separately.
A: Thank you Susan. On the face of it you seem to be coming down in favour of Scotland.
B: Yes, it does look that way. France comes top of the tax relief column, with Scotland a close second and Germany third when all the figures are taken into account. In the end, our final judgement also depends on how much weight we attach to these different factors. As I said at the beginning, there's no doubt that communication is a crucial factor. Maybe so much so that we should decide on Lyon and forget the other factors.
A: Now, wait a minute. Not too fast. What do the rest of you think?
C: I'd like to raise the question of profit versus cost centres. If we see the plant as a cost centre with our sales offices throughout Europe as profit centres, then tax becomes a less vital issue.
B: That may be true in the future, but it's not the way we're structured at present. At the moment each entity acts as a profit centre; however, through internal pricing we can take account of tax variations.
A: What do you mean, Susan?
B: Well, simply the rate at which one part of the company charges another part for the supply of goods or services – what the papers call transfer pricing.
A: Of course, that dreaded bogey!

2 Listening

Chart 6.8

	Communication	Labour force	Plant construction	Manufacturing cost	Tax benefits
Scotland	3	1	1	1	2
France	1	2=	2	2	1
Germany	2	2=	3	3	3

3 Comprehension/interpretation

3.1 Ease of supply and delivery.

3.2 Availability and skill.

3.3 Because they respond to the needs of sales departments, they do not have the opportunity to make profits.

3.4 By using transfer pricing.

4 Language focus

4.1 Questions – softening

1. Can I ask you about tax incentives?
2. I was wondering whether they offer help with incentives?
3. Could you tell me if the tax authorities advised you about transfer prices?
4. I wondered how much the land cost?
5. Could you tell me if you have included the tax weighting . . . ?
6. I was wondering what the rest of you think?
7. Would you mind telling me if you are thinking of siting . . . ?
8. Could you tell me why you won't consider Germany?

NOTE: These are only model questions; other versions are possible.

4.2 Clarifying

A: We've been trying hard to avoid double taxation?

B: What do you mean?

A: Well, simply paying tax twice – first in the country of payment and secondly in the country of residence.

B: So, if I understand you correctly, you are saying the expatriate workers could have to pay tax here in Saudi and again back in the US.

A: That's right. We have approached the US tax authorities and it seems there is a double taxation agreement between the two countries but it is time dependent . . .

B: Could you say that more slowly?

A: Of course, what I meant/was saying was that it is possible to avoid double taxation but it depends on how long the expatriate works in Saudi. Now most of our contracted workers are on short contract varying from 60 to 120 days. The US tax authorities are prepared to waive tax after six months.

B: So are you saying that our guys are going to have to pay tax twice?

A: Yes, but it could be redeemable i.e./in other words they could get the tax back later . . .

5 Word study

1. scores . . . personality
2. scores lower than/lags behind
3. is just behind . . . way ahead
4. not much to choose between
5. on top

UNIT 7
Valuation

Section A: New approaches to valuation

Part 1: The value of brands

2 *Reading*

In Chart 7.1:

   (i) Proactive financial management
  (ii) Forward-looking
 (iii) Medium-termism
  (iv) Relativity

3 *Comprehension/interpretation*

3.1   Bolstering balance sheets by ascribing value to brand portfolios.
3.2   Because it is being used to assess whether a brand is doing well without reference to future performance.
3.3   Being only concerned with short-term profits/results.
3.4   Because it is more difficult to quantify the results.
3.5   They both involve the investment of cash to achieve better results.
3.6   You could use supply/demand analysis to measure the effect of advertising expenditure.
3.7   It is too complicated for ready implementation.

4 *Language focus*

4.1   Modals – overview

A: Surely your brands must be worth more than that?
B: Well, it's very difficult to say. They may/could well be. However, we prefer to put it on the conservative side.
A: I must/have to say I find these figures hard to believe. After all, a company that wanted to create a brand would have to pay a fortune in advertising alone.
B: Yes, that's true but you cannot put a figure on brand creation – it depends on so many factors.
A: I agree, but we could calculate from a historical basis.
B: That's not the point. The real value is the long-term potential profits. How can you estimate them?
A: Well, you must have annual sales forecasts.
B: Of course, but if we're going to value them in the balance sheet, we must have a longer-term perspective.
A: In my opinion what you should do is take ten years' potential net income and . . .

4.2   Reporting

1. i   2. e   3. d   4. f   5. c   6. h   7. g   8. j   9. b   10. a

NOTE: Other answers are also possible.

5   *Word study*

1. bolster
2. discretionary
3. ingenious
4. ascribe
5. allocate
6. stems
7. tricks
8. appropriate
9. practicable
10. defray

Part 2: Forecasting future performance

Listening tapescript

I think we're all here now. So, I'd like to take a few minutes of your time to describe what I see as the likely developments with two major products. Now, as you know, Phison has been on the market now for more than ten years and there's no doubt that it's nearing the end of its productive life. The other product which I look after is Superphison, which, as I'm sure you are all aware, we launched last year and for which we all have great hopes. Now my objective today is to get us thinking about investment priorities for these two products over the next five or six years – hopefully, by doing this, we'll be able to maintain the sorts of profit level we have been used to in this division.

So, I'd like to look at these two products from two points of view: firstly turnover and secondly profit.

If you look at this graph here, you'll see that I've projected turnover not only for next year but also in the medium term, for the following five years. The broken line represents Phison, the dotted Superphison. On the vertical axis we have turnover up to a maximum of $120 million. As you can see, last year, turnover for Phison remained pretty stable at $120 million, this year we have started to see a steady decline so that by the end of the year we forecast only $70 million. Next year this downward trend is likely to continue, but not so steeply, so that by the end of next year turnover should stand at $60 million. I'll come to the reasons in a moment. For the subsequent five years, we predict a gradual decline so that at the end of the century, turnover should stand at about $20 million. Now, let's turn to Superphison. This was launched in the middle of last year and climbed rapidly to reach $20 million by the end of the year. This year we have seen this trend sustained – so much so that we anticipate annual turnover for the year to be $70 million – thereby cutting the Phison line as it descends at the end of this year. We have very clear and not surprising evidence that Phison's decline is largely accounted for by customers upgrading to Superphison. In other words, we have seen what we anticipated – a process of cannibalism. If we look into the near future: next year we see the upward trend in turnover continuing so that sales reach $100 million by the end of the year. All well and good. What is worrying is the steady decline which follows so that by the end of our forecast period Superphison is back down to $80 million. I'm sure you're all wondering why. The simple answer is that Superphison will no longer be competitive – and although we predict that some of our customers will be loyal, this number will be matched by those who turn to our competitors. Anyway, I'm sure we'll come back to this point later. Let me move on now to my second graph which shows profit growth and decline over the same period.

Again, on the horizontal axis we have the same time periods, whilst on the vertical axis we have a scale from zero to $22 million in profits. The curve for Phison is very similar to the turnover curve I've just shown you. At the end of last year profits stood at $22 million, over this year we see a rapid decline to just $12 million by the end of the year, there's a steadying of profits next year when we reckon that we will have made the necessary cuts in sales and production and profitability will be maintained – so that there's only a slight fall to $11 million at the end of next year. Over the following five years, we see a long steady decline down to $4 million by the end of the decade.

Meanwhile, Superphison started to make up for this shortfall in profits when it started earning money for us at the beginning of this year. We forecast $8 million by the end of the year. This unfortunately will be followed by a slight plateau as we invest in the dealer network as the product really takes off – so much so that we see profits level at $8 million by the end of next year. The following five years should show solid profit growth despite the downturn in sales – all our investment will have been made and we should be reaping the rewards. We expect profits to hit $20 million by the end of this five year period.

So, in conclusion, the message is clear. We need to be using the future profits of Superphison now to invest in new product development – certainly it'll mean tight conditions for a few years, but this is the only way we can ensure a solid future for this division.

2 Listening

Chart 7.2

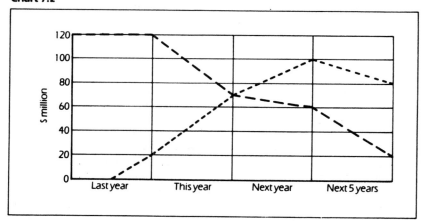

Chart 7.3

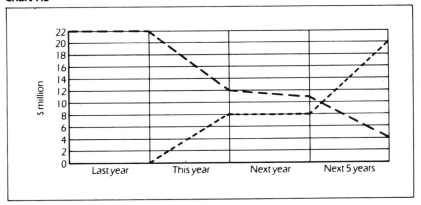

3 Comprehension/interpretation

3.1 The likely developments with two major products.
3.2 Customers have been upgrading to Superphison.
3.3 It will no longer be competitive.
3.4 The necessary cuts in sales and production have been made.
3.5 Because of investment in the dealer network..
3.6 We need to invest in new product development.

4 Language focus

4.1 Describing trends

1. e, h
2. d, g, i
3. b
4. c, f, l
5. a, j, k

4.2 Describing graphs

1. c   2. d   3. a   4. e   5. g   6. b   7. f

5 Word study

Figure 7.5   a, c, f, j, l
Figure 7.6   b, h, m, o
Figure 7.7   g, i, n
Figure 7.8   d
Figure 7.9   k
Figure 7.10   e

6 Transfer

B: (i) Listen to your partner's presentation of a graph. Use the information to recreate the same graph in Chart 7.11c.

(ii) Describe Chart 7.11d so that your partner can draw it.

Chart 7.11c

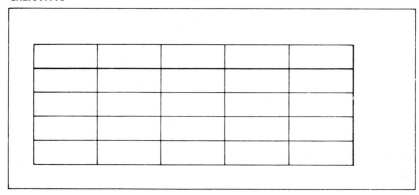

Chart 7.11d

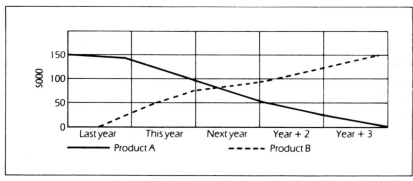

Section B: Company ratings and failure

Part 1: Valuation and business failure

2 Reading

Chart 7.12

	Colfield	Parkroll
Peak market value	£280m	£430m
Balance sheet gearing	8 → 35%	20–65%
Interest cover	8.5	4.5
Liquidity ratios	1.5 → 1.1	1.5 → 1.4
Operational cash flow	positive	positive
Dividends	15% increase	70% increase

3 Comprehension/interpretation

3.1 It indicates a company's ability to pay interest on its long-term loans.
3.2 Up to you! (1 is usually considered healthy)
3.3 It means making the accounts work in the company's interest.
3.4 Although it seems a reliable indicator, it can become a vicious circle, spiralling down as confidence is lost.
3.5 Up to you!

4 Language focus

4.1 Past time – past perfect

1. We didn't want to see the accounts because we had already seen them.
2. When the figures arrived, they had already been drafted twice.
3. The office was very quiet when I visited it. Everybody had gone home.
4. The company published some excellent results last year. Later, it went bust.
5. The company reported an upturn in profits last month. Earlier in the year, it had announced declining sales.
6. There were two major company collapses last week. Both companies had tried to avoid bankruptcy.

4.2 Too/both/either/neither

1. I think this company is going to go bust. – I do too.
2. He didn't think the results were good. I didn't either.
3. Both of us had invested in Parkroll. We both lost a lot of money.
4. Both companies grew rapidly. Neither controlled their growth.
5. Which company are you going to invest in? – Either, I don't really mind.
6. Which company are you going to invest in? – Neither, they are both in unstable markets.

5 Word study

Success	Failure
record profits	to go bust
strong growth	disaster
spectacular accounts	seeds of collapse
doubling of earnings	grounds for caution
healthy balance sheet	deterioration
at their peak	plunged horribly
positive cash flow	touching bottom
management confidence	collapsing share
	a burden of debt
	profit warning

Part 2: Discussion of privatisation

Listening tapescript

A: Good evening. We're here tonight to discuss the pros and cons of privatisation. As we all know, it's difficult to separate out the political, financial, industrial and social arguments which are put forward in favour of privatisation and just as vehemently opposed by those who see it as a form of asset stripping on a national scale.

On the political side, we have a government party which sets great store by increasing share ownership amongst the electorate and thereby spreading the benefits of popular capitalism. On the other hand, we have an opposition party which accuses the government of selling off the nation's silver at rock-bottom prices in order to tie the voter to the vested interests of the Tory party.

On the financial front, we have economists and analysts who claim the government has consistently under-priced the share value of public assets in order to secure a successful take-up of the shares by institutions and private investors which has done nothing to improve the financial position of these large national companies. In contrast, there are those who believe that water, telecommunications and gas, to name but three, have all been successful privatisation issues which have led to major restructuring and financing of these industries.

From an industrial point of view, we have heard from those who believe that privatisation is the only way to make traditional bureaucratic industries competitive. However, there are just as many who believe privatisation in some sectors has only changed public monopolies into private monopolies with no appreciable effect on competitive performance.

Finally, on the social side, is privatisation a necessary step towards creating a new entrepreneurial, non-bureaucratic society where we all have the opportunity to benefit from the pleasures of increased dividends or suffer the rigours of the market economy in the form of unemployment and factory closures? Or, are there certain key infrastructure industries such as telecommunications, power supply and railways which are better left in the hands of disinterested civil servants who are more likely to look after the futures of our children and grandchildren?

My apologies for such a lengthy introduction but that should set the scene. Peter Smythe, as opposition spokesman on trade and industry, can I ask you to start the discussion?

B: Certainly. I'd like to start by reminding you all of one of the so-called successes of privatisation – British Telecom. There's no doubt it's been a rip-roaring success for those lucky or acquisitive enough to lay their hands on the shares – I believe they've more than doubled since their issue – but that's not my main concern. The government has always held up privatisation as a means to greater competition and therefore efficiency, and thus better value for money for the customer. Judging by the level of complaints that I receive from my constituents, I see very little evidence of improved service. Maybe the large business customer gets quicker attention but the poor old residential customer somewhere out in a village in my constituency, who relies on the telephone as a lifeline, has seen no improvement, just increased prices.

A: I'm sure Simon Goodall, government spokesman would like to respond to that.

C: Yes, I certainly would. I happen to have a briefcase full of the latest quality of service measurements from British Telecom. I won't bore you with the details. Suffice it to say that on all fronts British Telecom have made great strides forward. They themselves admit that there's further room for improvement but I'm confident that we have a much better service now than five years ago, before privatisation.

B: All that proves is that you are as taken in as all the other viewers of BT's expensive television advertising campaign. I admit their public relations has improved enormously.

A: Right, gentlemen, perhaps we can move on. I wanted to ask Susan Crabtree of the Consumer Association . . .

2 Listening

Chart 7.13

	Arguments in favour	Arguments against
Political	Increase share ownership	Tying the voter to the Conservative party
Financial	Can lead to major restructing and financing of public sector industries	If under-priced, does nothing to improve financial position
Industrial	Makes bureaucratic national companies efficient	Changes public monopolies into private monopolies
Social	Creates a more entrepreneurial, non-bureaucratic society	Some essential industries are safer in the hands of disinterested civil servants

3 Comprehension/interpretation

3.1 Because the Tory (Conservative) party closely aligns itself with the interests of public and private companies.

3.2 Up to you!

3.3 Because they have a longer-term perspective – usually remaining civil servants all their working lives.

3.4 Those who bought shares.

3.5 Rural, residential electors.

3.6 Public relations hides a lack of improvement in the service.

4 Language focus

4.1 Presentations – introducing subjects

1. d   2. e   3. b   4. c   5. a

4.2 Relative clauses

1. There are twenty people waiting outside who have been invited to the show.
2. The government spokesman, who comes from the Finance Ministry, is going to speak on the programme.
3. Telecommunications, which was privatised six years ago, has always been very profitable.
4. The government, which was first elected eleven years ago, has followed a policy of privatisation.
5. Peter Smythe, who is an opposition spokesman on trade and industry, starts the discussion.

5 Word study

1. g   2. l   3. m   4. h   5. a   6. n   7. d   8. k   9. b   10. i   11. e
12. j   13. c   14. f

GLOSSARY

A

A shares (n) non-voting shares

absorb (v) to take in a smaller item to form part of a larger whole; *we can absorb the loss of the subsidiary*

acceptance (n) the act of agreeing to accept a bill of exchange

account (n) a record of financial transactions

> **accountancy** (n) work of an accountant

> **accountant** (n) person qualified to keep a company's accounts

> **accounts** (n) the financial records of a busines; *the bank would like to see the accounts*

accrual (n) gradual increase by addition

> **accruals** (n) money owed which is due at a later date

> **accrue** (v) to increase and to be due at a later date

acid ratio (n) ratio of current assets minus stock to current liabilities; used as a measure of solvency

acquire (v) to buy or obtain; *we acquired a company*

> **acquisition** (n)

actuary (n) a professional insurance official responsible for estimating future claims and premiums

advance 1. (n) money paid as a loan or part payment   2. (v) to lend money; *the bank advanced us £2000*

agent (n) a person authorised to carry out transactions on behalf of another person

allocate (v) to give money in certain proportions; *in the budget we allocated most of the money to marketing*

amortise (v) to pay off a debt by saving money on a regular basis; *the total cost can be amortised in five years*

annual (adj) for one year; *the annual accounts*

> **annual general meeting (AGM)** a meeting of all shareholders

anti-trust (adj) against monopolies; *anti-trust laws*

appropriate (v) to put a sum of money aside for a purpose

> **appropriation** (n) profit appropriation

arbitrage (n) buying shares in a company which is likely to be taken over

> **arbitrager** (n) person who buys and sells shares before and after a takeover

arrears (n) money which is owed and has not been paid on time

assess (v) to calculate the value of

> **assessment** (n) tax assessment; *my tax assessment is always wrong*

asset (n) something of value which is owned by a company

> **current assets** (n) assets in daily use by a business

> **fixed assets** (n) property and machinery

> **frozen assets** (n) assets which cannot be sold, usually because there is a dispute

> **intangible assets** (n) assets which cannot be seen (such as goodwill, patents, etc.)

> **liquid assets** (n) cash or bills which can be easily converted into cash

> **tangible assets** (n) assets which can be seen (such as property, machinery, etc.)

asset stripping (v) buying a company in order to sell its assets

attribute (v) to put a name to, to classify

> **attributable profits** (n) profits whose origin can be identified

audit (n) examination of the accounts of a company

> **auditing** (n) official process of checking the accounts of a company to see if they represent a true picture

> **auditor** (n) person who audits

authorised capital (n) amount of capital which a company is allowed to have

average (n) number which is representative of many figures; *the average inflation rate is 10 per cent*

B shares ordinary shares with special voting rights

back 1. (adj) referring to the past; *I am owed a lot of back pay* 2. (v) to support; *the bank refuses to back the project*

backdate (v) to put an earlier date on a document

backer (n) person/company who financially supports someone; *our American backers have pulled out of the project*

backing (n) financial support

back office (n) the department in a firm of stockbrokers which deals with settlement procedures

bad debt (n) debt which will not be paid

balance (n) amount which makes the total credits and debits equal

> **balance brought forward (bbf)** (n) amount entered at the start of an account which represents the balance from the last period

> **balance of payments** (n) international financial position of a country (account of imports, exports and invisible earnings)

balance sheet (n) statement of the financial position of a company or business at a certain moment

bank charges (n) charges a bank makes for services provided to a customer

bank draft (n) order by one bank to get another bank to pay money to someone

bank statement (n) written statement showing transactions and balance of an account

bankrupt (adj/noun) declared unable to pay debts and put in the hands of a receiver; *he was declared bankrupt*; *he went bankrupt*

> **bankrupt** (v) to force someone to become bankrupt; *they bankrupt my business*

> **bankruptcy** (n) state of being bankrupt

base rate (n) principal rate of interest charged by a bank

bearer (n) person who holds a cheque or certificate

bear market (n) period when share prices are falling

benchmark (n) point which can be used as a basis for comparison; *we have set a benchmark figure of 5 per cent*

bid (n) offer to buy something at a certain price; *takeover bid*

> **bidder** (n) person who makes an offer; *the company will go to the highest bidder*

bill (n) written paper promising to pay money

billion (n) GB: one million million; US: one thousand million

blank cheque (n) a signed cheque with no payee or amount

blue chips (n) shares with the highest status as investments – usually shares of well-established companies

bond (n) contract document promising to repay money borrowed by a company or government

bonus (n) extra payment; *we offer a Christmas bonus to all employees*

books (n) the financial records of a company

> **book value** (n) value of assets as recorded in the company's books

> **bookkeeper** (n) person who keeps the financial records of a company

boom (n) time when business activity is increasing; *we must take advantage of the economic boom*

borrow (v) to accept money from someone on the basis that you repay it later

bounce (v) referring to a cheque which is returned to the bearer because there is not enough money in the payer's account

break even (v) to balance costs and revenue, to not make a profit or a loss; *we just broke even last year*

breakeven point (n) point at which revenue equal costs

broke (adj informal) having no money; *he's broke until he receives his pay cheque*

       go broke (v) to become bankrupt; *the company went broke*

broker (n) person who buys and sells shares/currency

budget (n) plan of forecast income and expenditure

       The Budget (GB) annual plan of government spending and taxation

       budgetary (adj) referring to a budget; *budgetary control*

building society (n) (GB) financial institution which lends money to people buying property

bull market (n) period when share prices are rising

bust (adj informal) bankrupt; *the firm went bust*

buyout (n) **management** ~: takeover of a company by its managers and directors

call (n) demand to pay for new shares

       call option (n) option to buy shares at a certain price

capital (n) money, property and assets used in a business

       capital expenditure (n) money spent on fixed assets

       capital gains (n) money made on the sale of a fixed asset

       equity capital (n) amount of a company's capital owned by the shareholders

       risk capital (n) money for investment in risky projects

capitalisation (n) **market** ~: value of a company based on its total share value

carry forward (v) to take a balance forward from the last accounting period, usually abbreviated to c.f. in financial statements

cash 1. (n) money in notes and coins   2. (v) to exchange a cheque for cash

cash flow (n) cash coming in to a company in sales less the money going out in purchases and overheads

       negative cash flow (n) more money going out than coming in

       positive cash flow (n) more money coming in than going out

Chancellor of the Exchequer (n) British finance minister

charge 1. (n) money paid for a service; *a delivery charge*   2. (v) to ask someone to pay; *the bank charges their business customers 10p a cheque*

chartered accountant (n) accountant in UK who has passed professional examinations and is a member of the Institute of Chartered Accountants

cheque (n) (US: check) note ordering a bank to pay money to the person/company whose name is written on the cheque

claim 1. (n) request for money; *we put in an insurance claim after the accident*   2. (v) to ask for money; *we claimed $50,000 in damages*

Co. short for Company

collateral (n) synonym for security; *the bank wants to know what collateral we are offering against the loan*

collect (v) to make somebody pay their debts; *tax collection; tax collector*

commodity (n) goods sold in large quantities, e.g. raw materials such as metals, grain, sugar, etc.

company (n) a registered business

       company secretary (n) person responsible for the company's legal affairs

       limited (liability) company (Ltd) (n) a private company where the shareholders are responsible for repaying debts to the value of their shares

compound interest (n) interest which is added to the capital and then earns interest again

conglomerate (n) group of companies joined together producing different products

consolidate (v) to put the accounts of subsidiary companies into the parent company's accounts; *consolidated accounts*

consumables (n) bookkeeping item for goods which have a limited life

contingency (n) possible state of emergency; *a contingency fund has been set up in case of bankruptcy*

convert (v) to change money from one currency to another; *convertible currency*

    convertible stock (n) stock which can be exchanged for shares at a later date

corporate (adj) referring to the whole company

    corporation tax (n) tax on profits of a company

cost (n) amount of money which has to be paid

    cost-effective (adj) which gives value; *the scheme is cost-effective*

    costing (n) the calculation of costs for a project

    fixed costs (n) costs which do not increase when production increases or decreases

    running costs (n) costs of day-to-day management of a company

    variable costs (n) costs which increase or decrease as production changes

credit 1. (n) time given to a customer to pay; *we normally give 3 months' credit* 2. (v) to put money into someone's account

    credit control (n) checking that customers pay on time

    credit limit (n) a maximum amount that a customer can owe

    creditor (n) person who is owed money

    creditworthiness (n) ability to repay money borrowed

    creditworthy (adj) able to buy goods on credit

    credit rating (n) amount which a credit agency thinks a company/person should be allowed to borrow

    letter of credit (n) a note from a bank allowing credit and promising to repay at a later date

cross-holding (n) two companies holding shares in each other

cumulative (adj) which is added each year to the previous year's total; *cumulative interest*

currency (n) money which is used in a particular country

    hard currency (n) currency of a country with a stable economy

    soft currency (n) currency of a country with a weak economy

current (adj) referring to the present time

    current account (n) bank account from which a customer can withdraw money at any time without giving notice of withdrawal

    current assets (n) assets used by a company in its day-to-day running (materials, cask, etc.)

    current liabilities (n) debts which a company must repay in the short-term

damages (n) money claimed for harm done; *we are claiming damages for unfair dismissal*

day-to-day (adj) ordinary, happens regularly

DCF discounted cash flow

deal 1. (n) a business agreement; *we set up a deal with our agents* 2. (n) amount; *a great deal of money* 3. (v) to trade, buy and sell; *he deals in gold*

    dealer (n) person who buys and sells; *a foreign exchange dealer*

debenture (n) agreement to repay a debt with fixed interest with the company's assets as security

debit 1. (n) money which is owed; the debit column is the left-hand column in accounts 2. (v) charge, deduct; *to debit an account*

---

direct debit (n) money withdrawn automatically from a bank account for regular payments

debt (n) money owed; *to get into debt*; *to be out of debt*; *to pay off a debt*

    debtor (n) person who owes money

    aged debtors (n) companies that owe money listed according to age of debt

declare (v) to make an official statement; *the company declared interim profits of $20 million*

    declaration (n) an official statement; *a tax declaration*

deduct (v) to subtract from the total figure; *after deducting all the costs, we actually made a loss*

    deductible (adj) which can be deducted; *tax-deductible*

    deduction (n) subtraction from the total figure; *after deduction of tax*

default 1. (n) failure to meet the terms of a contract; *the company is in default on its capital repayments* 2. (v) to fail to meet the terms of a contract

defer (v) to put to a later date; *we have deferred payment until next year*

    deferred payments (n) payments postponed to a later date

deficit (n) amount by which expenditure is higher than income; *the accounts show a deficit*

deflate (v) to reduce economic activity by cutting the money supply

    deflation (n) reduction in the money supply intended to cause a drop in prices

    deflationary (adj) *we have introduced some deflationary measures*

defray (v) to provide money for costs; *the sponsor agreed to defray the travel costs*

degearing (n) a reduction in gearing of a company

demand (n) 1. asking for payment; *final demands were issued to all late payers* 2. need for products and services at a certain price; *we are having difficulty meeting demand*

deposit (n) 1. money in a bank account (usually earning interest; *we require seven days' notice of withdrawal on this deposit account* 2. money paid in advance in order to reserve a product

depreciate (v) to reduce the value of assets in the accounts over a certain time; *we depreciate business equipment over five years*

    depreciation (n) reduction in the value of an asset; *straight line depreciation is calculated by dividing the costs of the asset by the number of years of active use*

deregulation (n) reducing government control over industry

devalue (v) to reduce the value of a currency against other currencies

    devaluation (n) reduction in the value of a currency

disburse (v) to pay money

    disbursement (n) payment

discount 1. (n) percentage reduction in a full price 2. (v) to reduce the full price

    discount rate (n) the percentage taken when a bank buys bills

    discounted cash flow (DCF) calculating return on investment while taking into account present value of money

disinvest (v) to reduce investment by not replacing capital assets

divest (v) to sell assets; *we divested ourselves of our South American companies*

dividend (n) percentage of profits paid to shareholders

documentary credit (n) a letter of credit from a bank

draft (n) order for money to be paid by a bank; *a banker's draft*

due (adj) owed; *this debt became due last week*

earmark (v) to set aside for a special purpose; *we have earmarked $50,000 for promotion*

earn (v) to receive money for work

    earnings (v) salaries, profits, dividends, interest received

earnings per share dividends per share shown as a percentage of the market value of a
share

price/earnings ratio ratio between market price and current dividend

economic (adj) 1. provides enough money; *this project doesn't make economic sense* 2. referring
to state of the national economy; *there is an economic crisis*

economical (adj) saving money; *an economical car*

economics (n) study of macro- and microeconomics

economise (v) to save money

economist (n) person who specialises in the study of economics

economy (n) 1. not wasting money or resources; *we need to introduce some economies*
2. (n) financial state of a country; *a free market economy*

employ (v) to use (money; return on capital employed)

equity (n) right to receive dividends on the shares you own in a company.

equities (n) ordinary shares

equity capital (n) amount of a company's capital owned by the shareholders

Eurobond (n) a bond issued in a currency other than that of the country it is issued in

exchange (n) giving one thing for another; *exchange control; foreign exchange*

expenditure (n) amount of money spent; *capital expenditure is the money we have spent on fixed
assets*

expense (n) money spent; *we renovated the building at great expense; the salesman had
a generous expense account*

expenses (n) money paid for covering extra costs; *the fee did not include travel expenses*

F

factoring (n) business of taking on other people's debts

FIFO first in first out (inventory system)

finance 1. (n) money used by a company; *Where will we get the finance for this project?*

finances (n) money available; *the poor state of the company's finances* 2. (v) to provide
money for; *the bank is going to finance the new building*

financial (adj) referring to finance; *financial position*

financially (adv) to do with finance; *the company is financially dependent on one
shareholder*

financier (n) person who lends large sums of money

financing (n) the process of providing money

firm (n) a business or partnership; *a law firm*

fiscal (adj) referring to tax; *the government is using fiscal measures to slow down the economy*

float (v) to put a company's shares for sale on the stock exchange

flotation (n) *a new company flotation*

floating exchange rate (n) an exchange rate which is not fixed

foreclose (v) to force a company/person to sell assets in order to pay debts

forward (adj) in advance, to be paid later

forward buying (n) buying at today's prices for delivery later

fraud (n) making money by not telling the truth; *he became rich through systematic fraud*

fraudulent (adj) not honest

fund 1. (n) money set aside for a special purpose; *a pension fund* 2. (v) to provide money for; *we
funded the company in its early days*

funds (n) money available to spend; *we need extra funds to pay for research*

futures (n) trading in shares and commodities for delivery at a later date

G

gearing (n) ratio between a company's capital borrowed at fixed interest and the value of its ordinary shares

        highly-geared (adj) having a high proportion of fixed-interest loans

going (adj) active, running; *this business is a going concern*

gold standard (n) value of a currency in relation to the value of gold

goodwill (n) good reputation of a business – intangible asset connected to customer base, track record, etc.

gross (adj) total, with no deductions

        gross margin (n) percentage difference between sales and direct cost of sales

        gross profit (n) profit calculated as sales less direct cost of sales

        gross yield (n) profit from investment before tax deductions

group (n) several companies joined together; *the group profits were down on last year*

grow (v) to become larger; *our liabilities have grown rapidly*

        growth (n) increase in size

H

half-year (n) six months; *the first half-year was disappointing*

        half-yearly (adj) *it's time for our half-yearly meeting*

hand (n) **in-hand** ready; *cash-in-hand is kept in reserve for daily expenses*

handle (v) to deal with; *our bookkeeper handles all the figures*

hedge (n) protection, security; *we spread the loan as a hedge against interest rates*

        hedging (n) investing at a fixed price for delivery later

hidden (n) not declared, is not clear; *there are certain hidden costs*

hire-purchase (n) paying for something in regular instalments

historic(al) (adj) in the past

        historical cost (n) the actual cost when the item was purchased

hold (v) to own; *the chairman holds 45 per cent of the shares*

        holder (n) person who owns something; holders of shares in the company

        holdings (n) group of shares; *he has holdings throughout the Middle East*

        holding company (n) company which acts only as a legal entity for owning shares in subsidiary companies

hostile (adj) unfriendly; *a hostile takeover bid*

I

income (n) money received through operations or investment

        earned income (n) money earned through work

        unearned income (n) money received from investments

incorporate 1. (v) to include as part of the whole; *profits from the subsidiaries have been incorporated*   2. to register a company (US); *an incorporated company*

increment (n) regular increase; *I am due for an annual increment on my salary*

        incremental (adj) rising automatically in stages; *an incremental cost*

incur (v) to be liable for, to have to pay; *we have incurred heavy debts*

indebted (adj) owing money; *we are indebted to a financing house*

index (n) a statistical figure showing relative increase or decrease

> **index-linked** (adj) which is increased according to the retail price index; *an index-linked pension*
>
> **retail price index** (n) an indicator of the rate of inflation

indicator (n) something which is significant; *a key indicator is the inflation rate*

inflate (v) to increase

> **inflate the economy** (v) to activate the economy by increasing the money supply
>
> **inflation** (n) state of rising prices
>
> **inflation accounting** (n) allowing in accounts for the changing value of money
>
> **inflationary** (adj) resulting in an increase in inflation; *these wage demands will be inflationay*

insider dealing (n) illegal use of inside information to buy and sell shares (often before a takeover deal)

insolvent (adj) not able to pay debts; *the company will soon be insolvent*; insolvency (n)

intangible (adj) which cannot be seen or touched; *goodwill is an intangible asset*

interest (n) a percentage of the capital paid by a borrower to a lender; *interest rate* (n)

interim (n) half or part of the total period; *the interim report (6-monthly)*

inventory (n) stock; *we need to reduce our inventory*

invest (v) to put money into a bank, building society, shares or other project in order to earn interest/increase in value

> **investment** (n) money put into a bank or project etc. with the intention that it should increase in value
>
> **investor** (n) person who invests
>
> **safe investment** (n) a non-risky investment

invisible (adj) cannot be seen; *tourist economies have high invisible earnings*

invoice 1. (n) a note requesting payment   2. (v) to send an invoice to someone

irrevocable (adj) cannot be changed; an irrevocable letter of credit cannot be cancelled

issue (n) giving out shares

> **issued capital** (n) amount of capital held by shareholders
>
> **rights issue** (n) giving shareholders the right to buy new shares at a lower price
>
> **scrip issue** (n) free shares to shareholders

item (n) entry in accounts; *there's a new item on the balance sheet*

jobber (n) person who buys and sells shares from other traders on Stock Exchange; *jobbing* (v)

joint (adj) combined, shared between two parties

> **joint bank account** (n) bank account of two people
>
> **joint stock company** (n) public company with shares owned by many people

junk bonds (n) bonds raised as debentures against the security of a company about to be taken over

lame duck (n) company that needs financial support

lease (n) contract for renting property or equipment for a period of time

> **lease back** (v) to sell property or machinery and then take it back on a lease
>
> **lessee** (n) person who pays for a lease
>
> **lessor** (n) person who receives money for a lease

ledger (n) book in which accounts are written

    nominal ledger (n) record of a company's income and expenditure by named accounts, departments

    purchase ledge (n) record of expenditure

    sales ledger (n) record of sales

lend (v) to allow somebody to use your property

    lender (n) person who lends money

    lending (n) allowing someone to borrow money

leverage (n) ratio between capital borrowed and value of shares

    leveraged buyout (n) buying all the shares in a company using the value of the shares as security

levy 1. (n) money collected by the authorities; *there is an import levy on all non-EC produce* 2. (v) to demand payment of taxes and dues

liability (n) legal obligation; *our liability is limited*

liabilities (n) debts of a business

    current liabilities (n) short-term debts

licence (n) (US: license) official document which gives permission; *you need an import licence*

    licence (v) to give permission

    licensee (n) person who is given permission

    licensor (n) person who gives permission

LIFO last in first out (inventory system)

liquid (adj) easy to realise; *liquid assets*

    liquidity (n) having assets which can be converted into cash

    liquidity ratio (n) the ratio of current assets to current liabilities

liquidate (v) to close a company and sell its assets

    liquidation (n) process of closing a company; *the business went into liquidation*

    liquidator (n) person who supervises the liquidation of a company

listed (adj) registered; *shares can be bought in listed companies*

    listing (n) official list of companies whose shares can be bought or sold on the Stock Exchange

loan 1. (n) money which has been lent; *loan capital must be repaid at a later date* 2. (v) to lend

lose (v) to not make a profit; *we are losing money*

    loss (n) *we suffered a loss*

lump sum (n) money paid in one single amount; *you can pay in one lump sum or by instalments*

major (adj) important; *the major shareholder has 35 per cent of the shares*

    majority shareholding (n) more than 50 per cent of the shares

management accounts (n) financial information (sales, costs, profits, cash flow, etc) prepared for managers

margin (n) difference between income and costs

    gross margin (n) percentage difference between unit manufacturing cost and manufacturer's price

    marginal tax (n) percentage of tax paid at top rate

    net margin (n) percentage difference between all costs and manufacturer's price

market (n) place where products and services can be bought and sold

    capital market (n) place where companies can look for investment capital

market-maker (n) a broker-dealer who buys and sells securities and thus make a market for them

money market (n) place where money is traded

maximise (v) to make as large as possible; *we must maximise profits*

measure (n) action, step; *we are going to take measures to reduce costs*

merchant bank (n) financial institutions which carry out a range of services (historically not clearing banks)

merge (v) to join together; *the company merged with another European company*; *merger* (n)

minimise (v) to make something as small as possible; *we need to minimise costs*

monetary (adj) referring to money; *monetary policy was popular in the eighties*

monetarism (n) economic theory that inflation can be controlled by regulating the money supply

monetarist (n) person who supports the theory of monetarism

mortgage 1. (n) contract for buying a property using the property as security for a long-term loan
2. (v) to obtain a loan with a property as security; *the house is mortgaged*

N

negotiable (adj) can be negotiated, subject to agreement; *a negotiable bill can be freely transferred*

net (adj) after all deductions have been made; *net margin*; *net profit*

nominal (adj) as registered, as indicated; *the nominal value of the shares is much lower than the current market rate*

O

off-balance sheet (n) where an asset is acquired by leasing and not subject to depreciation

operational (adj) working, running; *the operational costs are too high*

option (n) the possibility, opportunity; *we have the first option to buy the property*

share option (n) right to buy/sell shares at a certain price on a future date

outgoings (n) money which is paid out, expenditure

outlay (n) expenditure; *the capital outlay exceeds our borrowing facility*

outright (adj) complete; *outright purchase*

outstanding (adj) not yet paid; *What is the amount outstanding on this account?*

overdraft (n) amount of money which a person/company withdraws from a bank account and which is more than is in the account

overdraft facility (n) arrangement with a bank for an overdraft to a certain limit; *our overdraft facility is £50,000*

overdraw (v) to take out more money from a bank account than is in the account

over-extend (v) to borrow more than you can pay back; *we have over-extended ourselves*

overhead (adj) day-to-day running and administrative; *our overhead costs have increased*

overheads (n) (US: overhead) non-attributable, running costs

over-the-counter (n) refers to unlisted stocks and shares

owe (v) to have to pay money; *they owe the bank £25,000*

par (adj) equal, standard

>**par value** (n) the printed value on a share certificate

>**above/below par** (n) market price above/below par value of a share

parent company (n) company which owns more than 50 per cent of the shares of another company

parity (n) exchange rate/equal value; *the French franc and the Swedish Krøner reached parity*

partnership (n) unregistered business where two or more people share risks and profits

pay 1. (n) money given for work or service   2. (v) to give money for work or service; *to pay tax*; *to pay by cheque/credit card*

>**take-home pay** (n) salary after deductions

payback (n) paying back money which has been borrowed or invested

>**payback period** (n) time for repayment or return on investment

PAYE Pay As You Earn: income tax deducted at source by the employer

payslip (n) note which shows salary and deductions

petty cash (n) small amount of notes and coins available in an office to pay for inexpensive items

place (v) to put

>**to place shares** to find a buyer for shares

plc public limited company

plough back (v) to reinvest; *all our profits have been ploughed back into the business*

point (n) 1. place or position; *we have reached breakeven point after the first year*   2. decimal point; *the dollar fell 2 points against the Deutschmark*

portfolio (n) a range, collection; *a portfolio of shares*

>**portfolio management** (n) buying/selling a range of shares for a client

power (n) strength

>**purchasing power** (n) a company's purchasing power can usually be gauged by the size of the discounts that it can obtain from its suppliers

preference shares (n) shares which have priority in dividend payment before ordinary shareholders – usually at a fixed rate of interest

premium (n) 1. extra charge; *these shares will sell at a premium – 10p above their face value*   2. price paid for insurance

price (n) money charged for something

>**asking price** (n) opening price in negotiation

prime (adj) best, most important; *the bank is offering its prime rate for investment*

profit (n) money gained from doing business

>**operating profit** (n) profits from normal trading of a company

>**profit and loss account** (n) accounts showing income and expenditure (US: income statement)

>**profitability** (n) ability to make a profit

>**profitable** (adj) which makes a profit

provision (n) money set aside in accounts for later use; *the banks have made a provision for bad debts*

public (adj) 1. referring to the government/state; *the government has increased public expenditure*   2. of a company whose shares can be bought on the Stock Exchange; *the company has decided to go public in order to raise the necessary capital*

purchase 1. (n) something which has been bought; *it will be cheaper to make a quantity purchase*   2. (v) to buy

quaterly (adj/adv) happening four times a year/every three months; *our quarterly results were excellent*

quota (n) fixed amount which is allowed; *there is an import quota on cars*

quote 1. (v) to estimate the value-cost; *could you quote for the contract in dollars* 2. (n) an estimate

   quotation (n) 1. estimate of cost 2. listing of the price of a share on the Stock Exchange

   quoted (adj) of shares/companies; shares which can be bought on the Stock Exchange

raid (n) **dawn** ~: buying a large number of shares in a company at the beginning of a day's share dealing

   raider (n) company/person who buys shares in a company before making a takeover bid

raise 1. (n) US: an increase in salary; *she asked for a raise* 2. (v) to increase; *we raised the dividend by 5 per cent* 3. (v) to obtain; *we are trying to raise $50,000 on the money market* 4. (v) to bring up in discussion; *we raised the question of prices at the board meeting*

rate (n) charge for service or work, or for loans; *fixed rate; interest rate; depreciation rate*

   going rate (n) market price

ratio (n) proportion of something compared with another thing; *our liquidity ratio is not healthy (current assets to current liabilities)*

realise (v) to sell for money; *the sale of the house realised $150,000*

receive (v) to get something

   accounts receivable (n) money owed to the company

   receiver (n) government official appointed to run a company in serious financial difficulty

   receivership (n) in the hands of a receiver; *the company was put into receivership*

reconcile (v) to make two accounts agree; *the bookkeeper reconciles the bank account and the sales and purchase ledger every month; bank reconciliation (n)*

recoup (v) to get back money; *we recouped our investment in two years*

recover (v) to get better after a downturn; *the stock market has not recovered since the big fall*

red (n) **in the red** showing a loss; *my bank account is always in the red*

reduce (v) to make smaller; *we need to reduce our prices*

redundancy (n) being no longer employed; *I received a good redundancy payment*

   redundant (adj) *to make somebody redundant*

refinance (v) to raise money to pay back an original loan

reflate (v) to stimulate the economy; *the government reflated the economy by reducing taxes*

reinvest (v) to invest again

relief (n) help, support; *we are hoping to get tax relief on the new investment*

remunerate (v) to pay someone for a service

repay (v) to pay back

   repayable (adj) *short-term loans are repayable within a year*

reserves (n) amount of money set aside from profits for a specific purpose

resources (n) source of supply of something; *our financial resources are limited*

result/s (n) profit or loss at the end of an accounting period; *we announced some good results for last year*

retained earnings (n) undistributed profits

return (n) profit from an investment; *What sort of return can we expect?*

   return on investment (ROI) (n) amount received relative to amount invested

revalue (v) to put a new value on something; *our freehold property must be revalued*
risk (n) chance of success or failure; *to take a risk*
        risk capital (n) venture capital; capital available for investment in risky but potentially highly profitable exercises
        risk-free investment (n) an investment that is certain to make a good return
        risky (adj) *that's a risky venture*
ROI return on investment
rough (adj) approximate; *this is just a rough calculation*
round (adj) correct to, say, the nearest 10 or 100; *in round figures, we can say £5,000*
        round up/down (v) to increase/decrease to a whole number
run (v) to manage/organise; *he runs two businesses*
        running 1. (adj) operating; *running costs*   2. (adj) continuing; *we keep a running total from day to day*   3. (adj) consecutively; *we have made a loss for two years running*

S

save (v) to keep, not spend money
        saver (n) person who saves
        savings (n) money saved
        savings bank (n) bank where your money earns interest
scrip (n) of an issue of shares; free shares to existing shareholders
securities (n) investments in stocks and shares
        gilt-edged securities (n) investments in British government stock
        the securities market (n) place where shares can be bought/sold
        security (n) guarantee that a debt will be repaid; *he borrowed using his house as security*
set against (v) to balance one group of figures against another; *we should be able to set some of the profits against tax*
set aside (v) to not use in the present; *we set aside a provision of $20,000*
set up (v) to start something; *we set up a new business*
settle (v) to agree (to pay); *we settled the account*
        settlement (n) payment of an account
share (n) a small part of a company's capital; *A shares; B shares; ordinary shares; preference shares*
        shareholder (n) person who owns shares
slump (n) rapid fall; *a slump in prices*
solvent (adj) having enough money to pay debts; *solvency* (n)
sound (adj) stable, strong; *the company is financially sound*
spot (n) immediate; *the spot rate gives prices for immediate delivery*
spread 1. (n) difference between selling and buying prices of shares   2. (v) to space out over a period of time; *Could we spread the repayments over two years?*
stag 1. (n) person who buys shares and then sells them immediately   2. (v) to buy a new issue of shares and then sell immediately
stagnant (adj) not moving, inactive; *the market is stagnant*
stock (n) 1. quantity of goods for sale; inventories   2. stocks and shares; shares in ordinary companies; stock often refers to fixed interest securities (loan stock – in US: bonds)
        stockbroker (n) person who buys and sells shares for clients
        stock controller (n) person who controls inventories
        stock exchange (n) a market in which securities are traded
subscribe to a new share issue to apply for shares
        subscription to a new share issue offering shares in a new company

subsidise (v) to help or support financially; *the government subsidises new investment in depressed areas*

subsidy (n) money given to support unprofitable enterprises

sundries (n) small items not named

supply 1. (n) providing something; *we are subject to the laws of supply and demand*   2. (v) to provide something

supplier (n) person/company which supplies

surcharge (n) extra charge

swap (n) an exchange; *a swap of securities involves exchanging one security for another of the same value*

T

tangible assets (n) assets which can be seen such as property, land, etc.

tariff (n) a tax on imports; *there is a tariff barrier around the EC*

tax 1. (n) money charged by the government or an official body to pay for services   2. (v) to make somebody pay tax

capital gains tax (n) tax on the profit made on the sale of assets

corporation tax (n) tax on profits

income tax (n) tax on personal income

taxable (adj) able to be taxed

tax allowance (n) part of income which is received tax-free

taxation (n) process of taxing

tax avoidance (n) trying to minimize tax legally

tax concession (n) allowing less tax to be paid

tax deductible (adj) referring to an expense that can be deducted from total profits thereby reducing the amount on which tax must be paid

tax evasion (n) trying to avoid tax illegally

tax loophole (n) legal means of not paying tax

tax relief (n) allowing tax-free income

value added tax (VAT) (n) tax on goods and services

tender 1. (n) offer for a contract at a certain price; *the purchaser invited tenders from three suppliers*   2. (v) to offer a price and conditions for a contract

threshold (n) limit; *the tax threshold for VAT registration is £30,000*

tie up (v) to invest long-term; *we have most of our capital tied up in dockland property*

tip (n) advice; *he gave me a tip about those shares*

trade 1. (n) business of buying and selling; *we depend on overseas trade*   2. (v) to buy and sell; *he trades in shares*

balance of trade (n) international trading position of a country

insider trading (n) illegal buying or selling of shares by employees of a company based on inside information

trading profit (n) gross income exceeds total costs

transaction (n) exchange of goods or services for money

transfer 1. (n) moving something to another place; *we credited your account by bank transfer*   2. (v) to move something from one place to another; *we transferred our money to the Cayman Islands*

transfer pricing (n) adjustment of prices on sales made between parts of a multinational company

treasurer (n) person who looks after finance and funds of a club, society or company (US)

treasury (n) government department which deals with a country's finance

treasury bill (n) bill of exchange sold by government at a discount with no interest

treasury bonds bonds issued by US government

trend (n) general development in a market, business; *there is a downward trend in inflation*

trough (n) low point in business cycle

trust (n) 1. management of funds or property for someone; *the family has set up a trust fund for the grandchildren*   2. (US) small group/cartel of companies which controls a market

       anti-trust laws (n) designed to break up monopolies and encourage competition

turnaround (n) making a company profitable again; *he achieved a complete turnaround in the company's fortunes*

turnover (n) 1. total amount of sales; *our turnover in 1991 was 25 per cent up on 1990*   2. speed/ regularity with which staff or stock change: *staff turnover; stock turnover*

under-capitalised (adj) not having enough capital

under-utilised (adj) not used enough; *much of the capital is under-utilised*

undistributed (adj) not distributed; *the undistributed profit was retained*

uneconomical (adj) which does not make a profit; *this project is uneconomical*

unissued (adj) not issued; *there is $500,000 of unissued capital*

unit (n) single item; the unit cost goes down as production increases

       unit trust (n) organisation which invests money in a variety of shares for small investors

unlisted (adj) not listed

       unlisted securities market (USM) market for buying and selling shares not listed on the Stock Exchange

unsecured (adj) with no security; *unsecured loan*

value 1. (n) amount of money something is worth; *the book value of the assets is lower than the real value*   2. (v) to estimate how much something is worth

       valuation (n) the act of valuing; *we carried out a stock valuation at the end of the year*

variable (adj) which changes; variable costs increase as production increases

variance (n) difference; *the budget variance shows the difference between forecast and actual results*

variation (n) amount something changes; *the sales are subject to seasonal variation*

variety (n) different types, range; *there is a variety of products to choose from*

vary (v) to differ, change; *the margin varies depending on raw material costs*

venture (n) risky business project; *we need venture capital to start*

viable (adj) can work/can be profitable; *this project is not viable*

       viability (n) ability to make a profit

visible (adj) can be seen; *visible trade figures exclude earnings from tourism*

wealth (n) amount of money and assets owned by someone

       wealthy (adj) rich

wind up (v) to close down a company; *the company was wound up with debts of $100,000*

window-dressing (n) financial adjustments to the accounts of a company so that they read better

withholding tax (n) tax deducted from payments to non-residents; *these dividend payments are subject to withholding tax*

working capital (n) the excess of current assets over current liabilities, sometimes called the current ratio

write down (v) to enter an asset in the books at a lower value than before

write off (v) to cancel/remove a debt from the accounts; *the debt has been written off*

        write-off (n) loss/cancellation of a bad debt

yield (n) the income from a security as a proportion of its market price; *current yield*; *dividend yield*